Alexander Dunmore

A frontier campaign 1897-1898

A narrative of the operations of the Malakand and Buner field forces. Second

Edition

Alexander Dunmore

A frontier campaign 1897-1898

A narrative of the operations of the Malakand and Buner field forces. Second Edition

ISBN/EAN: 9783337141844

Printed in Europe, USA, Canada, Australia, Japan

Cover: Foto ©ninafisch / pixelio.de

More available books at **www.hansebooks.com**

A
FRONTIER CAMPAIGN

A NARRATIVE OF THE OPERATIONS OF THE MALAKAND AND BUNER FIELD FORCES, 1897-1898

BY

THE VISCOUNT FINCASTLE, V.C.
LIEUTENANT, 16TH (QUEEN'S) LANCERS

AND

P. C. ELIOTT-LOCKHART
LIEUTENANT, "QUEEN'S OWN" CORPS OF GUIDES

WITH A MAP AND SIXTEEN ILLUSTRATIONS

SECOND EDITION

METHUEN & CO.
36 ESSEX STREET, W.C.
LONDON
1898

Colonial Library.

PREFACE

THE following pages are compiled, with the aid of the official despatches, from the rough diaries of two officers, who, belonging to different brigades of the force, were fortunate enough between them to witness the events described, with the exception of that portion of Chapter XII. which deals with the operations under Major-General Elles, C.B.

For many of the illustrations their thanks are due to Major Biddulph, 19th Bengal Lancers, Captain Hewett, Royal West Kent, and Lieutenant Dixon, 16th Lancers, who by their kind contributions have endeavoured to lend an interest to a book which otherwise is merely a plain record of the part taken by the Malakand and Buner Field Forces in the recent Frontier Campaign.

CONTENTS

CHAPTER I

                                                       PAGE

CAUSES OF THE OUTBREAK - - - - 11

CHAPTER II

THE MALAKAND — THE MAD MULLAH — NEWS OF A GATHERING IN THE SWAT VALLEY — ATTACK UP THE BUDDHIST ROAD — COLONEL MEIKLEJOHN'S SORTIE — A V.C. - - - 26

CHAPTER III

ARRIVAL OF THE GUIDES — EVACUATION OF NORTH CAMP — SEVERE FIGHTING IN THE CRATER CAMP — SYED AHMED SHAH — THE MULLAH WOUNDED — HIS REPUTED MIRACLES — ARRIVAL OF COLONEL REID'S COLUMN - 40

CHAPTER IV

FORMATION OF MALAKAND FIELD FORCE — AN UNSUCCESSFUL SORTIE — ARRIVAL OF SIR BINDON BLOOD — RELIEF OF CHAKDARA - 54

CHAPTER V

CHAKDARA FORT — ITS GARRISON — SIEGE — A PLUCKY RIDE — ARRIVAL OF THE RELIEVING FORCE - - - - - - - - 65

CONTENTS

CHAPTER VI

THE SWAT VALLEY—MARCH TO UPPER SWAT—LANDAKAI - - - - - - - - 79

CHAPTER VII

MINGAORA—THE SACRED VILLAGE OF SAIDU—RECONNAISSANCE TO MINGLAOR—BUDDHIST RUINS - - - - - - - - - 101

CHAPTER VIII

EXPEDITION AGAINST THE MOHMANDS—SEIZURE OF THE PANJKORA BRIDGE—MARCH THROUGH BAJOUR—NIGHT ATTACK ON SECOND BRIGADE 111

CHAPTER IX

PURSUIT OF THE ENEMY—INAYAT KILA—MARCH UP THE MAMUND VALLEY—SEVERE FIGHTING—DIFFICULTIES OF RETIREMENT - - 123

CHAPTER X

GENERAL JEFFREYS BENIGHTED—VILLAGE OF BILOT—HEAVY THUNDERSTORM—LOSSES IN THE MOUNTAIN BATTERY—PUNITIVE OPERATIONS - - - - - - - - - 135

CHAPTER XI

POSITION OF FIRST BRIGADE AT NAWAGAI—THE HADDA MULLAH—TWO NIGHT ATTACKS—GENERAL WODEHOUSE WOUNDED - - - 147

CONTENTS

CHAPTER XII

ARRIVAL OF GENERAL ELLES—CAPTURE OF THE BEDMANAI PASS—THROUGH THE JAROBI GORGE—THE HADDA MULLAH'S HOME BURNT—FURTHER OPERATIONS IN THE MAMUND VALLEY - - - - - 162

CHAPTER XIII

ATTACK ON AGRAH AND GAT—ARRIVAL OF FIELD BATTERY AND HIGHLAND LIGHT INFANTRY—SKIRMISH AT BADELAI—RAHIM SHAH - - 171

CHAPTER XIV

CESSATION OF HOSTILITIES — A DURBAR — DEPARTURE TO THE SALARZAI VALLEY — RECONNAISSANCE TO PASHAT—SUBMISSION OF TRIBES - - - - - - - 181

CHAPTER XV

COMMISSARIAT AND TRANSPORT ARRANGEMENTS—EXPEDITION INTO UTMAN KHEL COUNTRY—RETURN TO THE MALAKAND - - - 189

CHAPTER XVI

INVASION OF BUNER—ATTACK ON THE TANGI AND PIRSAI PASSES—PIR BABA ZIARAT—CLOSE OF THE CAMPAIGN - - - - 201

CHAPTER XVII

A RETROSPECT—THE BUNERWALS—MANNERS AND CUSTOMS—"WESH" - - - - 219

LIST OF ILLUSTRATIONS

	PAGE
PORTRAIT OF SIR BINDON BLOOD	*Frontispiece*
A FAKIR	28
TO ENCOURAGE THEIR FRIENDS	46
CAVALRY RECONNAISSANCE FROM MALAKAND	55
PURSUIT BY GUIDES, CAVALRY, AND 11TH BENGAL LANCERS IN THE RELIEF OF CHAKDARA	75
UPPER SWAT VALLEY	90
BUDDHIST STUPA SHANKARGHAR	109
KOH-I-MOHR, IN THE BAJOUR VALLEY	112
A SIKH ORDERLY	123
A MALIK IN THE MAMUND VALLEY	142
SHINDANA PASS	164
SKETCH OF ATTACK ON AGRAH AND GAT	174
SNIPING THE CAMP AT NIGHT	184
PASHAT, SALARZAI VALLEY	187
THE TANGI PASS. 7TH MOUNTAIN BATTERY IN ACTION	207
PIR BABA ZIARAT	217

CHAPTER I

CAUSES OF THE OUTBREAK

TO the ordinary observer there was nothing in the aspect of the political horizon on the 26th of July 1897 that presaged the storm of fanaticism which in a few hours was to sweep down the Swat Valley and hurl itself against our garrisons at Malakand and Chakdara. But our political officers, with their fingers on the pulse of these turbulent tribesmen, had been aware, ever since the Chitral expedition of 1895, of an under-current of fanatical agitation in the country north of the Peshawar district, but as mutual jealousies and intertribal dissensions had in no way been laid aside, there was nothing to indicate the near approach of a combined rising of the tribesmen against the supreme Government.

In searching for the causes which led up to this outbreak, it is necessary to briefly review the history and condition of affairs in the country during the last half-century, when the celebrated Akhund, or Frontier Pope as he has been styled by several writers, first rose to note. To this man's influence the extreme fanaticism of the Yuzafzai tribes of Swat, Buner, and the surrounding countries, may in a great measure be ascribed. But the Akhund, although spiritual leader in Swat, and therefore the head of all religious and fanatical movements, was an astute and far-seeing man, who, with the exception of the Ambéla Campaign in 1863, prevented the tribes under his influence from embroiling themselves with the British Government. In that year, it will be remembered, a British force, on its way through the Ambéla Pass to chastise a colony of Wahabi fanatics, commonly known as the Hindustani fanatics,

CAUSES OF THE OUTBREAK 13

living to the east of Buner,—found itself confronted by a strong force consisting of these same fanatics and most of the fighting strength of Buner. Owing to great pressure being brought to bear on him, the Akhund brought a contingent of tribesmen from Swat and the neighbouring districts to join this gathering. After very severe fighting, the tribesmen were defeated and a treaty was made between the British Government and the Swatis, in which the former undertook not to annex Swat, and the tribesmen to abstain from molesting our subjects or committing raids in British territory. With a few small exceptions, this treaty has been loyally adhered to by the Swatis for thirty-two years, and the Government has abstained from any interference in the country.

In April 1895, however, it became necessary to despatch Sir Robert Low's force through Lower Swat to save the hard-pressed garrison of Chitral, and the Government of India entered into negotiations with the Swatis, explaining the object of the despatch of troops through their country, which was the shortest and most expeditious route to follow. A proclamation was sent to the tribesmen stating that, if they abstained from opposing our troops, their country would not be annexed or interfered with, and their property would be carefully protected from damage.

This would not seem a very unreasonable request; but the presence in Swat of numerous fanatical Mullahs, who are everywhere violently hostile to the British, and the fanatical character of the tribesmen themselves, imbued with their innate love of independence and suspicion of our motives, made the fulfilment of a peaceable march through the country impossible, and the opposition at the Malakand Pass and subsequent actions at the Swat and Panjkora rivers were the result. After Chitral had been relieved, Lord Rosebery's Government came to the conclusion that the strategical importance of Chitral as a post of observa-

CAUSES OF THE OUTBREAK 15

tion near the passes over the Hindu Kush range in the event of further progression by the Russians had been exaggerated, and orders were issued for the withdrawal of the troops to British territory. Before this was effected, however, there was a change of Government, which resulted in a reversal of this decision, Chitral being retained, with a road through Swat and the Khan of Dir's territory as a link with India: this road having been completed before the 20th June 1895, on which date the orders of the Liberal Government to evacuate Chitral reached Sir Robert Low.

It does not come within the scope of this work to discuss the arguments for or against the retention of a distant post like Chitral, which can only be kept in communication with India by a road running through a belt of mountainous country, peopled by the most fanatical tribesmen on the Indian frontier. But as, for many reasons, Lord Salisbury's Government decided to retain Chitral, it was incumbent on the Government of India, especially as they had unanimously advised that course, to make the most suitable arrangements possible for the maintenance of a road to connect it with British territory.

At that time the only means of getting to Chitral lay by two routes from Rawal Pindi, both of them traversing high passes through a most bleak and mountainous country. Troops could either be sent from Rawal Pindi *via* Srinagar and the Gilgit road, a total distance of 647 miles, to Chitral; or *via* Abbottabad, Chilas and Gilgit, a distance of 481 miles. The route which was now decided on, while avoiding many of the difficulties of the former roads, was also far shorter, the distance from our border in the Peshawar District to Chitral being only 160 miles. In order to keep this road open for the passage of troops moving in relief, the Government purchased sufficient land to build our military posts on the Malakand Pass and to protect the bridge over the Swat river at Chakdara, and subsidised the Khan of Dir to protect and keep open the road through his territory, which was soon largely used by traders. The Khan of Dir * was left to govern his territory after his own methods, without interference from us; and, with the exception of the personal influence of the political authorities to put an end to factional fights calculated to endanger the safety of the road, the tribesmen of Swat were left to administer the country through their own tribal council.

Ever since 1895 and the opening of the Malakand cart-road there has been a great impetus to trade in Bajour, Dir and Swat, but the influence of a growing industry has not yet been sufficient to appreciably lessen the tribal jealousies which periodically break out into open hostilities; and lately the Nawab of Dir, finding the influence exerted over his own immediate subjects for disaffection by the fanatical party in Upper Swat on his border was rapidly becoming a serious matter, pro-

* Lately made a Nawab.

ceeded to Upper Swat to assert his authority. This move of the Nawab was a severe check to the fanatical party, and their chances of raising trouble in Dir, on the Chitral road, which must have appeared somewhat promising a month previously, were dissipated.

Their efforts, however, were successful in a quite unexpected quarter. The Mad Fakir, who had been discredited both in Buner and in Upper Swat, on his arrival at Thana, a village in Lower Swat, so worked on the passions of the people that when he proceeded down the valley they turned out *en masse*, carrying away the inhabitants of Aladand and other villages with them, and on the same evening commenced hostilities.

This decided move was a signal for people from all parts where fanaticism had been preached to come down and join in the attack, and in the course of a few days representatives had arrived from all tribes north of the Peshawar district between the Indus and Kunar rivers. There

CAUSES OF THE OUTBREAK

appeared to be an entire absence of premeditation in the first attack on the Malakand, but there is little doubt that the news of the fighting in the Tochi Valley, on the top of the widespread fanatical disaffection fostered by the Mullahs, had put the tribesmen on the alert for an opportunity of which they were not slow to avail themselves. The rising in Swat was quickly followed by attacks on our posts on the Mohmand border, in the Khyber Pass, and all along the border of the Kohat district up to the Kurram Valley, and the unrest reached down to Beluchistan, where it was only suppressed by the prompt action of the local authorities in arresting the leading men.

For so many tribes scattered over such a vast extent of country to rise almost simultaneously, and in most cases resign solid advantages in the shape of liberal subsidies given them by Government to ensure their good behaviour, shows the extraordinary enthusiasm aroused throughout the country, far and wide, by the stories circulated after the looting of the North Camp. The Government property captured on that occasion supported the wild rumours, which spread with marvellous rapidity throughout the tribes, that the Malakand had been captured and our garrison massacred.

Another belief that the tribesmen were firmly embued with, was that the Amir would support them, and there were many factors that lent colour to this supposition in the eyes of the people, among them being the titles which Abdur Rahman, in endeavouring to pose as the head of the Mohammedans of the East, had lately assumed, such as "King of Islam" and "Light of the Faith." He had also published pamphlets on religion which were decidedly of a nature to foment trouble and disturbances among such a fanatical race. One of these pamphlets, written some ten years ago, shortly after the Penjdeh incident, on the spiritual advantages of a 'Jehad" or crusade against the infidel, has lately been widely circulated both in Afghanistan and among the tribes on our frontier.

This pamphlet, signed as it was by the Amir himself, was quite enough for the Mullahs to impress the people with the idea that he would help them, although there is little doubt that the Amir originally wrote it to clear himself of the imputation put upon him by the Mullahs of being himself an infidel; and it expatiates on the advantages to a Mohammedan of waging war against infidels in general, and not against us in particular.

The state of the feeling of the population both of India and Afghanistan for the last few years may be described as one of intense religious excitement and enthusiasm. In India both Hindus and Mohammedans have been affected by it, and it is to be regretted that the numerous band of semi-educated political malcontents have seized on it to redouble their tirades in the native papers against the Government, and represent every action of the authorities as directed against the interests and liberties, religious or otherwise, of the ignorant population. Under an exceptionally pure and unselfish administration, it would appear strange that there should exist such a large body of disaffected individuals, and it is only when we remember that, before we became paramount in India the country was split up into numerous states, which for the most part disappeared as we advanced, and as the map of India (as Ranjit Singh described it) became red, that it will appear natural that some of the descendants of the rulers of these submerged states should bear us ill-will. A notable instance of this was shown during the Mutiny by the Nana Sahib, a descendant of the Peshwa of Poona; and other instances could be given, but they only account for a very small part of the discontented class. The remainder consist partly of a noisy body of men who have been imperfectly educated in the Government institutions, and who have failed to obtain service under Government, and partly of religious enthusiasts and members of the many religious and secret societies, whose discontent finds an opening through the native Press, which, since the repeal of Lord Lytton's Press Act, has been allowed absolute freedom.

Among the many factors in India which tend to sedition and intrigue, education,—in bringing the priesthood of the country into opposition to a progress which usurps its privileges,—may be said to play at least a minor part. Both Brahmins and Mullahs recognise that secular education in Government and Missionary Schools is tending to break down old superstitions and to produce a generation of free thinkers, who will no longer be content to remain under the yoke of the priests.

Moreover, education, which has advanced with giant strides of late years, has, with the learning to read and write, caused a corresponding amount of interest to be taken in the affairs of the world, and the news of the success of the Turks over the Greeks in the late war has undoubtedly had its effect on Mohammedan feeling among the populace in India. The unemployed loafer, who twenty years ago might have listened to the seditious preaching of a stump orator, now hears the latest news from Thessaly or the Soudan being read out from the papers, framed with the embellishments of a disloyal editor. Any success of the Turks or Arabs is hailed as a success of the Faith, and there has been a general idea in India lately that England, instead of being a firm ally of the Turks, as she undoubtedly was in the Crimean war, has joined the other Christian Powers in their desire to crush Turkey and deprive her of her conquests in Greece.

From the disloyal newspapers of Indian cities and their readers to the hills of the North-West Frontier is no far cry. News travels with marvellous rapidity in India, and with so many malcontents ready to stir up and foment trouble against the British Government, and the whole of the Afghan

CAUSES OF THE OUTBREAK

tribes on our border seething with fanaticism, it is not surprising that the rising tide should find an outlet at our weakest point; where the people, ignorant and priest-ridden to an amazing degree, are, through the medium of their Mullahs, an ever-ready instrument to the hand of intrigue and sedition.

CHAPTER II

THE MALAKAND—THE MAD MULLAH—NEWS OF A GATHERING IN THE SWAT VALLEY—ATTACK UP THE BUDDHIST ROAD—COLONEL MEIKLEJOHN'S SORTIE—A V.C.

IN the year 1895, in accordance with the policy to be pursued in keeping open the road between India and Chitral, a strong post was established on the Malakand Pass. At the time of the outbreak of the fanatical rising which led to the events which it is proposed to describe in this volume, the pass was held by a brigade consisting of three regiments of native infantry, a battery of mountain artillery, a squadron of native cavalry, and a company of sappers and miners; the entire force being under the command of Colonel Meiklejohn, C.B., C.M.G.

The Malakand is some thirty-two miles from Mardan, with which place it is connected by a metalled road constructed after the campaign of 1895. This road runs down through part of the Lower Swat Valley, crossing the Swat river at Chakdara, where a fort had been constructed for the defence of the bridge. The position occupied by the Malakand garrison was a somewhat extended one: the north camp on the left of the position being nearly three-quarters of a mile from the Crater Camp in the centre. A strong fort, some nine hundred feet above the Crater Camp, effectually holds the pass.

During the eighteen months that had elapsed since the occupation of the pass by our troops, life at the Malakand had flowed in the ordinary channels of a frontier post; leave was given to officers who could be spared from their duties, and the remainder of the garrison occupied their leisure hours with polo and other amusements. The 26th of July opened with no more eventful occurrences in prospect than the ordinary routine of the preceding months; it was little suspected that the apparent calm was to be so soon and so rudely disturbed. It is true that those whose business it was to watch the inner workings of the surrounding tribes had been conscious of elements of unrest. Reports had been received by Major Deane, the Political Officer of the station, that a fanatical Mullah had established himself in Upper Swat, and had gradually been gaining some influence over the inhabitants of the valley. This Fakir, who is now commonly known as the "Mad Mullah," originally came from Buner, and had planted his standard at Landakai. His success in attracting a following at first appeared doubtful, but on the 26th matters suddenly assumed a more alarming and disquieting aspect. The information received by the Political Officer was to the effect that the Mullah was advancing through Swat with an apparently increasing following. He was giving out that he had been

A FAKIR

inspired to preach a "Jehad" or Holy War against the unbelievers, and the derision with which he was at first received by the people was changed to awe and admiration when they saw him boldly pushing forward with his meagre retinue against a powerful enemy. With great shrewdness, he affected to be independent of all earthly assistance, and declared that he placed his sole reliance in the Heavenly Host, who were fighting on his side.

The boldness of his advance soon fired the latent fanaticism of the people, and by the time he reached Thana, the principal village of Lower Swat, the wave of religious enthusiasm swept all before it. Young men and old women, and even children, flocked to the standard of the leader under whose direction they were to be conducted to victory, to gain rich loot in this world or attain Paradise in the next. On the receipt of the news of the advance, Colonel Meiklejohn at once summoned the guides, cavalry and infantry from Mardan to reinforce the brigade, and all precautions were taken to repel the impending attack. The officers commanding the various corps were warned, and all necessary dispositions were in progress, when at 7 P.M. further news was received that the Fakir and his army had already arrived at Aladand. It was then considered advisable that a force should be detached to seize and hold the Amandara defile—a low "kotal" or pass commanding the road to Chakdara, about five miles from the Malakand. Orders were accordingly issued for a small column to start at midnight to effect this purpose, under the command of Colonel M'Rae, 45th Sikhs, while it was Colonel Meiklejohn's intention to move out at daybreak with the remainder of his brigade to disperse the enemy. The astonishing rapidity, however, of the movements of the tribesmen, and the astounding manner in which their numbers grew, rendered these intended movements impossible.

At 9.45 a telegram was received from Chakdara, to the effect that the tribesmen were moving in large bodies down the valley, evidently with the intention of attacking the Malakand. Almost immediately after its receipt, the wire was cut; at 10 P.M. a Jemadar (or non-commissioned officer) of the Local Levies came in with the news that the Fakir had reached Khar, a village only three miles distant from the Malakand, and that the hills to the east were at that moment swarming with men of his following. So swiftly had the course of events run that there was but little time to turn out and repel the attack. The "alarm' was at once sounded. The troops hastened to their posts, and they had hardly occupied these before the first shots rang out which heralded the onslaught, which continued night and day, with but slight intermission, for the next five days.

The first attack of the enemy came from the direction of the Buddhist road, which was discovered by our troops in 1895, at the storming of the Malakand. This road is on the right flank of the camp, and, where it reaches the top of the pass, runs through a narrow gorge. On the alarm sounding, Colonel M'Rae despatched Major Taylor, with a party of Sikhs, to secure this gorge, following himself, almost immediately afterwards, with a few reinforcements. Seizing their accoutrements, the Sikhs dashed up, to find themselves only just in time, for had the enemy penetrated the gorge, it is doubtful if our men could have withstood the onslaught of the hordes of tribesmen that would have poured on to our lines. As it was, the fire of our men was sufficient to check them temporarily; but the enemy soon scaled the rocks on either side of the gorge, and rolled down enormous masses of stone, while some poured in a hot fire at close quarters which rendered our position untenable.

The remainder of the 45th Sikhs now arrived, and, taking up a position some fifty yards in rear, Colonel M'Rae retired on them, and held this position all night, in spite of the great odds with which he had to contend. Before this move took place, several of the small handful of men who held the gorge had been killed and wounded, among the latter being Major Taylor, who, shot through the body, died almost immediately. Had it not been for the prompt action of Colonel M'Rae and the gallant behaviour of his little band, the upper portion of the camp would have certainly been rushed, and would probably have resulted in the massacre of all outside the fort. The advance of the enemy in this direction was now effectually checked, as none of them could brave the deadly fire of the Sikhs, who from time to time raised the old Sikh war-cry, whereby to intimidate the enemy and make them believe our men to be in greater force than they really were.

In the meantime, a large body of the tribesmen had advanced up the road from Khar and attacked the Crater Camp, in which were No. 5 Company Madras Sappers and Miners and the Field Engineer Park. A hand-to-hand conflict took place, in which the overwhelming numbers of the enemy soon overpowered our piquets and overran the native bazaar within our lines, where they killed all who were unable to escape and obtained a certain amount of loot. Some of the enemy penetrated into the Commissariat godown, killing the Commissariat officer, Honorary-Lieutenant Manley, who, with Sergeant Harrington, occupied a small mud hut in the centre of the enclosure. Sergeant Harrington had a marvellous escape from being killed as well as his companion; for the enemy, on entering the hut, cut down Manley, who tried to oppose them at the door, and then commenced feeling round the room in the dark for his companion, who heard one of them remark, "There ought to be two of them in here." Sergeant Harrington, being unarmed, stood perfectly still, and owing to the darkness and their eagerness to loot the remainder of the bazaar, the enemy failed to find him and left the hut.

Events had now taken a very serious turn. The Crater Camp was surrounded by tribesmen, who, under cover of the tents and bazaar huts, were able to creep up and charge our defences, which were manned by the Sappers and 24th Punjab Infantry, at close quarters. Within the Sappers' enclosure Colonel Meiklejohn and his staff stood with a company of the 24th, under Lieutenant Climo, ready to reinforce any part of our line of defence that should be hard pressed; while a place more or less sheltered from the enemy's fire was now marked out for our wounded, who, by this time, were fairly numerous. Among the officers, Major Herbert was the first to be laid out in this spot, having been shot through the leg, the bullet first passing through Colonel Meiklejohn's gaiter. Colonel Lamb, while stooping to lift Herbert up, received a dangerous wound through the thigh, from which he eventually succumbed;

and Lieutenant Watling of the Sappers was shortly afterwards brought in wounded from the quarter-guard, which he reported had been rushed and captured by the enemy.

On receipt of this bad news a party was hastily collected together, and, led by Colonel Meiklejohn in person, an attempt was made to retake the post. About thirty yards from the quarter-guard, however, a number of the enemy were found holding a cook-house, and in the hand-to-hand struggle which ensued Colonel Meiklejohn's small party was forced back some ten yards, where a stand was made until reinforcements could be obtained. In this melée several casualties occurred; Colonel Meiklejohn received a sword-cut on the neck, which, fortunately for him, had in the confusion of the struggle been delivered with the back of the sword, and resulted in nothing worse than a bruise; while Captain Holland was shot through the back, the bullet entering and coming out on one side of the spine, and then doing likewise on the other side, making four holes in its course. He was carried back to the enclosure by Climo, who afterwards returned with ten or twelve men to Colonel Meiklejohn's assistance. Thus reinforced, the party were able to reach the quarter-guard, the enemy being driven out at the point of the bayonet.

All that night our garrison were employed in repelling the tribesmen who tried hard to force an entrance, and the sounds of distant firing and the glare of star shell in the direction of the North Camp plainly showed that an attack was also going on there. Shortly before dawn the sounds of drums and serenais, which latter instrument is something similar to the bagpipes, were heard on the road leading from the valley, which showed that the enemy were being reinforced by fresh bodies of men. It was therefore decided to obtain reinforcements from the fort, as the men holding the Crater Camp had been fighting all night, and were still hard pressed.

Lieutenant Rawlins, 24th Punjab Infantry, was accordingly sent off with three sepoys to bring back some further troops. With so many of the enemy about, it was by no means a pleasant journey, and *en route* a Ghazi, who had crawled along unperceived in the darkness, jumped up close to him and tried to cut him down, but the prompt discharge of a couple of revolver bullets anticipated his intentions, and Rawlins accomplished his mission without further adventures.

It would be strange indeed if, with so much hard fighting, instances of individual pluck and heroism should not occasionally arise; and on this night, among the many deeds of which both British and Native might well be proud, was one which was shortly afterwards rewarded by a well-earned Victoria Cross.

A company of the 24th Punjab Infantry, who had been ordered to clear the ground up to the bazaar wall, had shortly afterwards been withdrawn into the inner enclosure.

Owing to the darkness and the confusion of the engagement, a havildar* of the company was left behind, badly wounded, his absence not being noticed for about two hours, until, a lull in the firing occurring, his cries for help could be heard. Lieutenant Costello of this regiment at once made a dash to the wounded man's assistance, followed by two of his sepoys, and in spite of the ground being at that time overrun by the enemy, and moreover swept by our own fire, succeeded in bringing him in safely. It was only owing to the darkness that this small party were able to carry out their desperate venture.

* Corresponds to "sergeant."

CHAPTER III

ARRIVAL OF THE GUIDES — EVACUATION OF NORTH CAMP — SEVERE FIGHTING IN THE CRATER CAMP — SYED AHMED SHAH — THE MULLAH WOUNDED — HIS REPUTED MIRACLES — ARRIVAL OF COLONEL REID'S COLUMN

THE next morning news was received from the North Camp. It appeared that they had been attacked by small parties only of the enemy, who had kept up a desultory fire all night without inflicting much damage, the tribesmen having evidently concentrated their efforts on the attack of the South Malakand and Crater Camp, although the North Camp, in its isolated position, offered a more tempting objective.

As soon as there was sufficient light, and

the bazaar had been cleared of the enemy, most of whom, it was found, had already decamped after having first massacred the bunniahs and native shopkeepers, Colonel Meiklejohn determined to push out in pursuit of the enemy. A column, composed of two battalions of infantry, a couple of guns, and a squadron of cavalry was accordingly ordered to proceed towards the Amandara Pass. These troops had gone but a very short distance up the valley before a large gathering of the enemy was seen advancing up the road. Major Gibbs, in command of the column, was at once ordered to return, and, as it was evident that the North Camp could no longer be safely held, all the tents and stores were ordered up with the troops, who were directed to concentrate in the Crater Camp. Many of the tents at the North Camp were too heavy for mule transport, and, as no camels were available and time was short, the tents had unfortunately to be abandoned, much to the delight of the enemy, who, swarming round the retiring force, at once carried off as many of the tents and as much of the baggage as possible, burning the remainder the same evening.

All that day large bodies of the tribesmen, with gaily-coloured standards, could be seen in all directions advancing over the hills to reinforce their comrades, who, by this time, occupied the heights, with their steep crags and peaks, which surround the Malakand, taking care, so long as daylight lasted, to keep out of range of our mountain guns, and it was evident that the attack on the previous night would be repeated in greater force on the coming one. The outbreak had now resolved itself into a combined rising of most of the neighbouring country.

The retirement from the North Camp to the Crater was completed in perfect order, under cover of the fire of the 24th Punjab Infantry and Guides Cavalry, the latter regiment having arrived from Mardan just in time to take part in these operations, and

ARRIVAL OF THE GUIDES 43

the last of the troops reached the Crater Camp shortly before dark.

The enemy had already commenced operations. One of our piquets had been rushed and overpowered by a large body of tribesmen, who held the post until Climo, with a couple of companies behind him, turned them out at the point of the bayonet, killing nine of them and capturing a standard. Meanwhile the Guides Infantry had arrived: a welcome addition to the garrison. They had received their orders while the officers were at mess the evening before, and, leaving Mardan at 1.45 A.M., arrived at the Malakand at 5.45 P.M., thus covering a distance of thirty-two miles in sixteen hours.

The conditions under which this march was made were most trying. The road from Mardan is for the greater part entirely destitute of shade or water, and the last seven miles, being a steady climb to a height of some 2000 feet above the plain, made it most exhausting to the troops, who were marching at the hottest period of an Indian summer.

In spite of their fatigue, the men arrived fit and full of keenness for a fight, a desire that was soon to be fully satisfied; for rest or sleep was a luxury which the garrison were unable to experience for some time to come. The enemy began their attack at 8 P.M., commencing with a vigorous assault on a small "serai" or fortified enclosure, at the N.E. corner of the Crater Camp.

This was held by twenty-five men of the 31st Punjab Infantry under a native officer, Subadar Syed Ahmed Shah. He and his small garrison made a most gallant and obstinate defence, and it was only when the tribesmen had succeeded in cutting their way through the wall, and setting fire to the door, that they were forced to evacuate it; which they accomplished by means of a ladder, with which they let themselves down over the wall on the side nearest to camp, to which they retired, fighting every yard of the way, hampered with their wounded,

ARRIVAL OF THE GUIDES

all of whom they succeeded in bringing in. Out of this gallant little band of one native officer and twenty-five men, nine were killed and ten wounded, including the native officer.

Some severe fighting meanwhile took place on the right flank, which was held by piquets of the 45th Sikhs and Guides Infantry. One piquet, consisting of twenty-five men from each of these regiments, was so hard pressed that at one time the enemy succeeded in effecting an entrance, to be turned out again shortly afterwards at the point of the bayonet. Of this piquet alone four men were killed and seventeen wounded.

Much the same sort of fighting took place on the left flank, where, during a sharp brush with the enemy, Costello received a severe wound, a bullet penetrating his back and coming out through the right arm; despite this he continued to do duty.

It was a veritable pandemonium that would seem to have been let loose around us. Bands of Ghazis, worked up by their religious enthusiasm into a frenzy of fanatical excitement, would charge our breastworks again and again, leaving their dead in scores after each repulse, while those of their comrades who were unarmed would encourage their efforts by shouting with much beating of tom-toms and other musical instruments. Amidst the discordant din which raged around, we could even distinguish bugle-calls, evidently sounded by some *soi-disant* bugler of our native army. As he suddenly collapsed in the middle of the "officers' mess call," we concluded that a bullet had brought him to an untimely end.

At daybreak a counter-attack was made which effectually cleared the nearer heights to the west of our position, the enemy being followed up in their retreat by a company of the 24th, under Climo, who inflicted great loss on them. This taught the tribesmen a lesson, causing them in future to retire before dawn to the shelter

TO ENCOURAGE THEIR FRIENDS

ARRIVAL OF THE GUIDES

of the neighbouring hills. A desultory fire was kept up all day from the tribesmen on our troops who were busy strengthening our defences and demolishing the bazaar and serai, which it was now determined to abandon. Trees were cut down to strengthen the abattis, and a wire entanglement and other obstacles were placed around the Crater Camp.

No rest was to be allowed to the hard-worked garrison, as towards evening the enemy could be seen swarming down the hills to the attack, while the white, dusty road leading up from the Swat Valley was completely hidden by the dark, sombre-clad figures of the Bunerwals, who, attracted by the wild rumours of a successful raid having taken place on the North Camp, had now arrived to partake in the capture and loot of the Malakand.

The assault commenced as soon as darkness set in, and the whole night was passed in hard fighting, the brunt of it falling on the 31st Punjab Infantry. This regiment had two officers wounded, Lieutenants Ford and Swinley, the former of whom would undoubtedly have bled to death had it not been for Surgeon-Lieutenant Hugo, who held the severed arteries together for several hours, thus saving his life.

The Guides Cavalry also nearly lost an officer on this occasion—Lieutenant Maclean (who was afterwards killed at Landakai), who had been sent to help the 31st Punjab Infantry owing to their paucity of British officers; he was wounded by a man who had crept up under the breastwork and discharged a pistol at him from a distance of about two yards. The bullet entered Maclean's face and came out under his ear: a truly wonderful escape.

Towards morning the attack died away and the enemy again retired into the hills, pursuing the same tactics as on the previous day. Some portions of the serai which had been left intact were now mined by the Sappers, the intention being to blow them up at night should the enemy occupy them. These mines were so constructed that they could be fired by a friction tube connected with the camp by a long wire.

During the attack which ensued that night these mines proved the greatest success, for, the enemy having collected in the serai preparatory to making an assault on our lines, Lieutenant Robertson, R.E., who had laid the mines, seized on the opportunity and exploded one. The deafening roar of the explosion and the noise made by the falling rocks was succeeded by an ominous silence: not a sound could be heard from the enemy, and there is little doubt that they received a considerable shock, if nothing worse.

The attack ceased at about 3 A.M., and daylight showed us the enemy carrying off their dead and wounded. During all this fighting, a good deal of it hand-to-hand, our forces had necessarily suffered considerable loss. The number of the officers was being reduced day by day, some of the regiments being particularly unfortunate in this respect. The 24th Punjab Infantry was now commanded by Lieutenant Climo, having already had three officers placed *hors de combat*. During the last assault by the enemy, Costello had been severely wounded for the second time, and Lieutenant Wynter, R.A., had been shot in the ankle.

Four days had now gone by since the first attack—four days and nights of almost continuous fighting, and the garrison were worn out with fatigue; while the enemy, still daily increasing in spite of their heavy losses, were firmly convinced that they would eventually take the Malakand. During the previous night they had attempted to make terms with the Afridi company of the 24th Punjab Infantry, proposing that they should come over to their side with their rifles and ammunition, and in return be given a share of the loot when the position fell into their hands. Our Afridis sent a well-directed volley by way of reply, and further negotiations ceased.

ARRIVAL OF THE GUIDES

This day, the 30th, was so far the quietest the garrison had experienced. The enemy were doubtless fully occupied in burying their dead, for their losses on the previous night had probably exceeded any that they had hitherto undergone. It was reported that the "Mad Fakir," who had personally led the attack, had been severely wounded, while another influential Mullah, who was his chief support, had been killed. Their Mullah being wounded evidently had a disheartening effect on the tribesmen, for, although they attacked as usual, their assault was delivered with far less vigour than on the previous night. It was stated that before going into battle the Mullah had given out that he would turn our bullets into water, thus by divine interposition rendering them harmless; and the extraordinary credulity and ignorance of the people is well exemplified in their implicit belief in his assertions.

Amongst the many miracles with which he was credited was one which bears a close resemblance to a well-known Biblical instance. Every man of his following brought him daily a handful of rice, as is the custom when visiting a holy man. Of this, the Mullah, with considerable acumen, took advantage, stating that he would feed his followers, who numbered several thousands, out of the contents of a small jar which he kept outside his abode, and it apparently never occurred to the people that they were but receiving back their own offerings.

Much to our discomfort, a severe duststorm broke over our camp in the middle of the night; this was followed by thunder and torrents of rain, and, at the height of the storm, the enemy tried to rush the 45th Sikhs' piquets, being repulsed, however, with great loss. We had now to remain in our wet clothes until day broke and the enemy had withdrawn.

The next day Colonel Reid's column, consisting of the 35th Sikhs and 38th Dogras, arrived, after a fearful march. On

ARRIVAL OF THE GUIDES

receipt of the news of the attack on the Malakand, Colonel Reid, who was then at Rawal Pindi, had been ordered with these two regiments to march at once to the relief. He arrived at Dargai with the 38th Dogras on the evening of the 29th, the men being terribly knocked up with the heat, which, even at night, was so oppressive that sleep was practically impossible. The crowded serai at Dargai presented a curious spectacle at dawn; camels, cavalry horses, mules and bullocks mixed up with bales of compressed forage and every variety of commissariat stores. The 35th Sikhs marched into Dargai early on the 30th, many of them so overcome by the heat that they succumbed immediately after their arrival. There was no ice, and the only water available was lukewarm, and these stalwart Sikhs, nineteen of whom died, lay scattered about in every stage of heat apoplexy.

CHAPTER IV

FORMATION OF MALAKAND FIELD FORCE—AN UNSUCCESSFUL SORTIE—ARRIVAL OF SIR BINDON BLOOD—RELIEF OF CHAKDARA

NEWS from the beleaguered garrison was meanwhile anxiously looked for in all parts of India, and, while the troops aforementioned were being sent up to the Malakand as fast as possible, Government proceeded to organise a relief force. No time was lost. On the 30th July the following order was officially published :—

"The Governor-General in Council sanctions the despatch of a force, to be styled the Malakand Field Force, for the purpose of holding the Malakand and the adjacent posts, and operating against the neighbouring tribes as may be required."

UNIV. OF
CALIFORNIA

CAVALRY RECONAISSANCE FROM MALAKAND

THE RELIEF OF CHAKDARA

Brigadier-General Sir Bindon Blood,* K.C.B., was appointed to the command of this force, being given the local rank of Major-General. Receiving his orders at Agrah on the evening of the 28th July, Sir Bindon Blood immediately started, and took over command at Nowshera on the 31st. At Mardan, the next day, he received a telegram from headquarters informing him that Chakdara Fort was hard pressed and running short of ammunition and supplies. On receipt of this news he pushed on with all speed, arriving at the Malakand about noon on the 1st August.

This same day, Colonel Meiklejohn had decided on making a sortie, for the Malakand garrison, having been reinforced by Colonel Reid's column, was now in a position to make a counter-attack on the enemy. Orders were accordingly issued for a reconnaissance to be made towards Chakdara, grave apprehensions being enter-

---

* Sir Bindon Blood served as Chief of the Staff to Major-General Sir Robert Low in the Chitral Campaign of 1895.

tained for the safety of the small garrison of that fort, from which no message had been received since the 30th.

The Guides Cavalry, and 11th Bengal Lancers, under Colonel Adams, were ordered to push forward if possible to Amandara, about five miles distant, and hold that pass until the infantry should arrive. But the advanced patrol, under Captain Baldwin, D.S.O., found the enemy in such force beyond the North Camp that it was clearly impossible to proceed without infantry to clear the way, the ground being impracticable for cavalry to operate over, a fact the enemy soon realised. The cavalry were therefore obliged to retire across the North Camp, closely followed by numbers of the tribesmen, who tried to work round their flanks and cut them off. In spite of the greater part of the ground being covered with rocks and intersected by ravines, several short charges were made with great effect, owing to the recklessness with which the tribesmen would occasionally advance over open ground. During one of these charges Baldwin received a severe cut on the head, Colonel Adams had his horse shot dead under him, while Keyes, a subaltern in the Guides, was slashed across the back by a Ghazi, who, in the excitement of the fight, fortunately delivered the cut with the back instead of the edge of his sword. An order was now sent to the cavalry to return to the Malakand, on which they retired up a narrow road leading from the North Camp to the Crater. This was not accomplished without difficulty, as the path, up which the cavalry could only proceed in single file, was exposed the whole distance to the fire of the enemy, who, taking advantage of every rock and stone, hovered round their flanks, pouring in a deadly fire, until Major Ramsay arrived with the 35th Punjab Infantry. On turning them out of these rocks this regiment killed twenty of them, capturing two standards and three rifles.

In the face of such strong opposition as this reconnaissance had proved was to be met, it was now too late in the day to attempt to push a force through to Chakdara. Sir Bindon Blood had meanwhile arrived and taken over command from Colonel Meiklejohn, and he, having decided that the small garrison of Chakdara must be relieved at all costs the following day, issued orders for a force to be ready to start at daybreak.

In pursuance of this plan, a column under Colonel (now Brigadier-General) Meiklejohn was ordered to bivouac on the open space known as "Gretna Green"; to advance the next morning down the road towards Chakdara, while a force under Colonel Goldney advanced up the hills to the right, and turned the enemy's flank. This scheme was afterwards carried out with complete success.

The relief force consisted of—

 400 Rifles, 24th Punjab Infantry, under Major Ramsay.

THE RELIEF OF CHAKDARA 59

400 Rifles, 45th Sikhs, under Colonel H. A. Sawyer.

200 Rifles, Guides Infantry, under Lieutenant P. C. Eliott Lockhart.

⎫
2 Squadrons, Guides Cavalry, under Lieutenant G. D. Smith, 2nd Central India Horse.

2 Squadrons, 11th Bengal Lancers, under Major S. B. Beatson.
⎭
The whole under Lieutenant-Colonel Adams.

4 Guns, No. 8 Bengal Mountain Battery, under Captain A. H. C. Birch, R.A.

50 Sappers, No. 5 Company Queen's Own Sappers and Miners, under Lieutenant A. R. Winsloe, R.E.

2 Sections Native Field Hospital, under Surgeon-Captain H. F. Whitechurch, V.C., I.M.S.

Colonel Goldney's force consisted of 250 Rifles of the 35th Sikhs, under Colonel Bradshaw, and 50 Rifles of the 38th Dogras, under Captain Stainforth. His attack was supported by two guns of No. 8 Bengal Mountain Battery.

At 4.30 A.M. Sir Bindon Blood, having ascertained that General Meiklejohn's force was ready to move off, passed an order to Colonel Goldney to advance, while he himself took up a position on Castle Rock Hill, whence he could superintend the operations generally. On receipt of the General's order, Colonel Goldney advanced silently towards the enemy's position, who, taken unawares, were completely routed, leaving many of their dead on the field. Owing to the success of this movement, the heights commanding the road leading into the valley were now in our hands, and consequently General Meiklejohn was enabled to march without opposition to the junction of the two roads, where the country, opening out, enabled him to deploy his force and attack the enemy under easier circumstances.

It was still dark when this column started, every man with his bayonet fixed, and not a sound was to be heard except the muffled tramp of feet on the dusty road, and the occasional clink of some portion of a mule's harness. The enemy was expected at every turn of the road, but, owing to Colonel Goldney's attack on the right, no opposition was met with until the lower valley was reached. Dawn was just breaking when a few shots were fired into the head of the column: these were the enemy's scouts put out to watch our movements, and, pushing on, we found the enemy had taken up a strong position close to where the road to the North Camp joins the main road leading down the valley. The enemy, from among the rocks and crags of a low hill, immediately opened fire on our advanced guard, on which General Meiklejohn, who was at the head of the column, ordered some of the Guides and 45th Sikhs to take the position at the point of the bayonet. Our men at once charged up the hill, the Guides Afridi Company giving vent to a wild yell, which ought to have gone some way towards intimidating the enemy, who, however, stuck to their position with the utmost tenacity, fighting like wild beasts at bay, until they were bayoneted among the boulders and rocks where they had made their stand.

The remainder of the Guides, together

with the 35th and 45th Sikhs, meanwhile stormed some "sungars" or stone breastworks on the rocky knolls to the left, where the enemy, with waving standards and yells of abuse and derision, awaited our troops. The fight, while it lasted, was a stubborn one, the enemy being determined to at least delay the advance; but our men, pushing their way pluckily up the steep slopes, slowly gained the heights step by step, and, in spite of the hot fire opened on them from above and the avalanches of rocks and stones which poured down the cliffs, succeeded in routing the enemy out of their stronghold, seventy or more being bayoneted or shot down before they could escape. On this the enemy lost heart, and were soon to be seen streaming up the valley in every direction, affording a splendid opportunity to our cavalry, who, quick to avail themselves of it, dashed in among the panic-stricken tribesmen, pursuing them without a check for over three miles, and the numerous bodies which strewed the

THE RELIEF OF CHAKDARA 63

route bore witness to the splendid execution done by lance and sword.

About three miles beyond Khar, some of the enemy were found to be holding the village of Butkheyla, but these were speedily cleared out by the infantry, and at the Amandara defile there was practically no opposition, only a few shots being fired at our cavalry as they hurried through, eager to reach Chakdara Fort, which, in the distance, presented the appearance of being on fire, so thick was the cloud of smoke which hung over it, and from which direction the rattle of musketry, varied by the dull report of the 9-pounder gun, clearly indicated that the gallant little garrison were having a hard time of it.

During the six days'* fighting which had taken place at the Malakand, our casualties were 173 of all ranks killed and wounded. This included 13 British officers and 7 native officers.

* 26th July to 1st August.

The following are the names of the British officers :—

KILLED

Major Taylor, 45th Sikhs.
Lieutenant Manley (Deputy Assistant Commissary).

WOUNDED

Lieutenant-Colonel J. Lamb, 24th Punjab Infantry (since died of his wounds).
Major L. Herbert, Deputy Assistant Adjutant-General.
Captain G. M. Baldwin, D.S.O., Guides Cavalry.
Captain H. F. Holland, 24th Punjab Infantry.
Lieutenant F. A. Wynter, Royal Artillery.
Lieutenant F. W. Watling, Royal Engineers.
Lieutenant E. W. Costello, 24th Punjab Infantry.
Lieutenant H. B. Ford, 31st Punjab Infantry.
Lieutenant H. L. S. Maclean, Guides Cavalry.
2nd Lieutenant C. V. Keyes, Guides Cavalry.
2nd Lieutenant G. D. Swinley, 31st Punjab Infantry.

CHAPTER V

CHAKDARA FORT — ITS GARRISON — SIEGE — A PLUCKY RIDE — ARRIVAL OF THE RELIEVING FORCE

IN the meantime the small fort at Chakdara was undergoing a vigorous siege at the hands of the enemy, who, on Monday the 26th (the same evening as they attacked the Malakand) had sent a force of about a thousand strong to invest this place. The garrison at this time consisted of two companies 45th Sikhs, under Lieutenant Rattray, who commanded the fort, Lieutenant Wheatley of the same regiment, twenty sabres of the 11th Bengal Lancers, Surgeon-Captain Hugo and Lieutenant Minchin of the 25th Punjab Infantry. Rattray having already been warned to be in readiness for an outbreak, which was considered possible, though not probable, had taken all precautions to safeguard the bridge, which would naturally be the chief point of attack; but it was not till the evening, while he was playing polo at Khar, that one of his men brought him the first intimation of the rumoured disturbance.

This news was brought in by a havildar, who reported that the tribes were rising, and that some of them whom he had met *en route* had taken from him his instruments and money. Rattray and Minchin both rode back to the fort through gradually increasing crowds of natives, who, strangely enough, allowed these two officers to pass unharmed through their midst, although a few hours later these same men were engaged in a desperate and fanatical assault on our posts.

At 10.15 that night a fire on a near hill, lit by one of the friendly Dir levies, warned the garrison of the near approach of the enemy, who attacked almost immediately on

CHAKDARA FORT

the west side of the fort. This was followed up by several rushes, as, being provided with ladders, they attempted to gain an entrance into the inner enclosure, but in each case were easily repulsed. About 4 A.M. they drew off, and occupied the heights which on the north-west side command the interior communications of the fort, and from the cover which these rocks afforded them they attempted to pick off the garrison.

The same morning Captain Baker, Transport Officer, and forty sabres of the 11th Bengal Lancers, under Captain Wright, arrived. They had left the Malakand at dawn, and though the hills which skirt the first part of the road were swarming with the enemy, Wright ordered a dash to be made for it, and reached the open ground below with no casualties. A mile or so farther on the road ran through a narrow defile, an impossible place to force with the cavalry at his disposal, and any attempt to penetrate would have meant the loss of the greater part of his men and horses. It was a matter of necessity, however, to get through to Chakdara, and in any case, retreat to the Malakand would by this time have been impossible; so, perceiving that he could not possibly get through the defile, he made for the river, and before the enemy had fully realised his intention, had got round the end of the spur by a rocky goat track; and the enemy, scrambling down the rocks in vast numbers to intercept the squadron, as it filed round the end of the hill, were too late to do any damage.

Half-way round the hill his advance was barred by a back water of the river; this he had to cross twice, swimming his horses. Two sowars were wounded here, and his hospital assistant nearly came to an untimely end through his being mounted on a small pony, which was swept off its legs and drowned. After passing Amandara his advance was unopposed, and he rode straight on to Chakdara, where he was a

CHAKDARA FORT

welcome addition to the not over-strong garrison of this place. On his arrival, Wright took over command.

The whole of this day was spent in repelling rushes of the enemy, who, having destroyed the telegraph line and surrounded the fort, had made communication with the Malakand almost impossible. Fortunately they were still able, under cover of the fire of the Maxim and nine-pounder, to convey food and water to their comrades in the signal tower; but the time approached when even this was to be stopped, and the small handful of men, cut off from all communication with the fort, were shortly to be confronted by the grim alternative of death by starvation and thirst, or at the hands of a cruel and implacable enemy.

By this time the tribesmen, ever impressionable and impulsive as children, had been worked up by the discordant din of their own tom-toms to the highest pitch of fanatical frenzy, and occasionally from out of the shifting crowd that swarmed over the slopes of the adjacent hills, a small body of wild-looking Ghazis, drunk with anticipated success, would dash up to the walls of the fort, there to meet with that death which, coming from the hands of the infidel, qualified them for an immediate entrance into the joys of Paradise.

One of Hugo's bheesties, who had deserted from the hospital a few days before the rising took place, used to get beneath the walls of the fort, under cover of the darkness, and shout abuse at our officers, evidently taking great delight in enumerating the tortures they would shortly undergo at his hands.

During the intervals of fighting, strenuous efforts were made to provide efficient head cover from the incessant sniping which the enemy were able to keep up from the adjacent heights, and the results which were attained under the clever expedients of Captain Baker must have been the means of saving many lives.

During the next few days and nights

the garrison were unable to leave their posts or to obtain any rest, for by this time there were hardly enough men to defend the parapets, some of them having been placed on the bridge below to prevent the enemy setting fire to it, which they tried to do by floating burning rafts down the stream from the opposite bank. A few of our men on the bridge, however, kept the enemy from approaching the river from that direction, no cover fortunately being available for them.

There was now no communication with the Malakand, from which direction could be heard heavy firing. The enemy made their most vigorous attacks under cover of the darkness, when the Maxim and nine-pounder were practically useless, and on the evening of the 29th they were seen approaching the signal tower, in largely increased numbers, with ladders and bundles of grass. These bundles of dry grass they placed at the foot of a shed or "lean-to" composed of wood and thatch, which, being propped up against the side of the fort, they intended to set fire to and thus burn the garrison out; but the Sikhs, by placing the muzzles of their rifles against this shed, succeeded in blowing it down, and thus rendered all their attempts futile. This tower was attacked all night without success, and the next morning some forty corpses were counted outside it. A misfortune now befell the Maxim, which had hitherto been held in great respect by the tribesmen, in that the foresight was shot away by a chance bullet; but apparently the temporary sight which was subsequently rigged up enabled this gun to undergo the remainder of the siege without much loss of prestige.

On the Friday a lull occurred, the enemy not advancing till the evening. This rest was badly wanted by the garrison, who were worn out with fatigue and want of sleep. The next morning, supplies and water were sent up to the men in the signal tower for the last time, as the enemy now held the ground between them and the fort, occupying the Civil Hospital, a building some way below the signal tower, from where they were able to fire with complete impunity into the outer enclosure of the fort, and several other bits of ground between our posts were found to afford them cover from our bullets. The hospital they proceeded at once to loophole on the side facing our position. The enemy's strength had by now been greatly augmented, while a far larger proportion of them were armed with rifles; and their marksmen on the ridge made it extremely dangerous to move about in the fort, all the most important interior communications being swept by their fire.

Matters, indeed, looked so serious, that it was decided to send an urgent appeal for help; but, owing to the danger and difficulty of signalling, it was only possible to send the two words "Help us" to the Malakand. To accomplish this a sepoy had to climb out of the port-hole of the tower carrying a helio, with which he proceeded to send the message, being exposed the whole time to the enemy's fire. The small garrison in the signal tower were, at the same time, sending urgent signals for water, which it was impossible to supply.

The following morning the enemy attacked at daybreak. They came on in the most determined manner, evidently resolved to take the fort at any cost before it could be relieved, and as they numbered from eight to ten thousand, their losses under the heavy fire from our guns were enormous. Ladders and bundles of grass, the latter to enable them to cross the wire entanglements which surrounded the fort, were carried by their storming parties.

Several of our men were killed, and the position was getting decidedly critical when the cavalry of the relieving column appeared over the ridge at Amandara, about four miles distant on the opposite side of the river. When these approached the bridge, the enemy began making off in small parties, on which Rattray with ten men made a

UNIV. OF
CALIFORNIA

PURSUIT BY GUIDES, CAVALRY, AND 11TH BENGAL LANCERS IN THE RELIEF OF CHAKDARA

CHAKDARA FORT

sortie against the hospital, which was then held by about thirty of the enemy. These soon fled, and Rattray pursued them for half a mile down the river, being joined *en route* by Baker and Wheatley with a small reinforcement. On their return, they found the cavalry checked by some Ghazis holding the Sangars on the hill, so these they also stormed, attacking them in flank, and driving them out at the point of the bayonet. In this encounter Rattray was severely wounded, being shot through the neck, and of his small handful of men, who so gallantly followed him, two were killed and one wounded. Over fifty bodies of the enemy were afterwards found on this hill.

While this was going on, the cavalry of the relieving force had pursued the enemy across the plain to the north of the fort, cutting off many fugitives; but, owing to their horses being done up and the heavy ground over which they had to pursue, they were obliged to return after going a comparatively short distance.

Thus ended the defence of Chakdara, after six nights and days perpetual fighting on the part of this small and plucky garrison against an overwhelming force. The way in which a few men defended the signal tower for the latter part of the siege, without water or any hopes of obtaining any, shows the stuff our Sikhs are made of. The strain of remaining at their posts for so many days, obliged to be always on the alert against an enemy, maddened by fanaticism, and increasing daily, was calculated to try the nerve of the staunchest soldier. Had the relief been delayed another twenty-four hours, the signal tower must have been abandoned owing to want of water. This would have rendered the fort practically untenable, owing to the heavy fire the defenders would have been exposed to from the high ground which the enemy could have then occupied. The sortie led by Rattray makes a brilliant finish to the gallant record of this small garrison.

After all necessary arrangements had been made, General Meiklejohn and his force bivouacked outside the fort at Chakdara and marched back next morning to Amandara, where they were met by Sir Bindon Blood, escorted by 500 Rifles under Colonel Reid. A further quantity of supplies and ammunition having been sent on to the fort, Sir Bindon proceeded to take this force up the valley to the villages of Thana and Aladand, which were thoroughly searched. No enemy being seen, the force bivouacked that night at Aladand, returning to the Malakand the following morning, with the exception of General Meiklejohn, who halted at Amandara to hold the defile and organise his brigade.

During these operations, the patient courage of our mule drivers and other followers—who behaved under the somewhat exciting circumstances of the morning of the 2nd August as if they were taking part in a peaceful field day in the plains of India—shows the implicit confidence these poor natives place in us, especially when we consider the scenes they had witnessed for nearly a week, shut up at the Malakand, and surrounded by a horde of wild barbarians thirsting for their blood.

CHAPTER VI

THE SWAT VALLEY—MARCH TO UPPER SWAT —LANDAKAI

THE crisis was now over. The tribesmen had all dispersed to their various homes, and were engaged in the peaceful occupation of reaping their crops, the greater part of them probably under the delusion that, owing to the distance and difficulties of marching troops at this time of year, they would escape punishment and enjoy a well-earned rest until a more favourable opportunity should arise for exterminating the infidel. There is no doubt that this opportunity would have occurred during the following spring, when the reliefs are sent up to Chitral. These reliefs consist of two regiments and two guns, with the stores and ammunition for the ensuing year, and the danger incurred by this small force, which has to protect a line of transport over eight miles long for a distance of a hundred and thirty miles through mountainous country, threatened on either flank by strong and well-armed tribes, may well be imagined. The road is kept open by the Khan of Dir's levies, but recent events have shown that, in the event of a tribal rising, no reliance could be placed on these gentry.

The next few days were spent by Sir Bindon Blood in organising the force at his disposal. The Malakand was put in order, and cleared of the debris and rubbish which had accumulated during the recent fighting. An advanced depot was installed at Khar, about three miles from the Malakand, and the troops which were to form the Second Brigade were moved there, thus relieving the overcrowded state which the hurried despatch of troops to the Malakand had caused. There were two Brigades mobilised in the Swat Valley. The First

THE SWAT VALLEY

Brigade, under Brigadier-General Meiklejohn, C.B., C.M.G.,* was now ready to march

* FIRST BRIGADE.

1st Battalion Royal West Kent Regiment.
24th (Punjab) Regiment of Bengal Infantry.
31st (Punjab) Regiment of Bengal Infantry.
45th (Rattray's Sikh) Regiment of Bengal Infantry.
Sections A and B of No. 1 British Field Hospital.
No. 38 Native Field Hospital.
Sections A and B of No. 50 Native Field Hospital.

SECOND BRIGADE.

1st Battalion East Kent Regiment.
35th (Sikh) Regiment of Bengal Infantry.
38th (Dogra) Regiment of Bengal Infantry.
Guides Infantry.
Sections C and D of No. 1 British Field Hospital.
No. 37 Native Field Hospital.
Sections C and D of No. 50 Native Field Hospital.

DIVISIONAL TROOPS.

4 Squadrons 11th Regiment of Bengal Lancers ("Prince of Wales' Own").
1 Squadron 10th Regiment of Bengal Lancers ("Duke of Cambridge's Own").
Guides Cavalry.
22nd Punjab Regiment of Bengal Infantry.
2 Companies 21st Punjab Regiment of Bengal Infantry.
10th Field Battery.
6 Guns No. 1 British Mountain Battery.
6 Guns No. 7 British Mountain Battery.
6 Guns No. 8 (Bengal) Mountain Battery.
No. 5 Company, Madras Sappers and Miners.
No. 3 Company, Bombay Sappers and Miners.
Section B of No. 13 British Field Hospital.
Sections A and B of No. 35 Native Field Hospital.

F

without tents and with ten days' supplies, as soon as instructions should be received from Simla as to future operations. The Second Brigade, under Brigadier-General Jeffreys, C.B., held a strong strategical position at Khar, on the bank of the Swat River, where they were within easy reach of the Malakand and Chakdara. The Malakand garrison was placed under the command of Colonel Reid, 29th Punjab Infantry, and the reserve brigade, which had been concentrated at Mardan under Brigadier-General Wodehouse, C.B., C.M.G., was formed into the Third Brigade Malakand Field Force, and shortly moved to Rustam, whence they could watch the passes into Buner, and from their presence on that side of the country prevent the Bunerwals joining the Upper Swatis *en masse* to oppose us.

The country between the Malakand and Chakdara was still strewn with corpses, which we were speedily burying; for, although these tribes are very careful to

THE SWAT VALLEY

carry away their dead, they had been unable to do so during our advance to relieve Chakdara. In several cases we found bodies tied between two bamboos, which form their primitive stretchers. No Red Cross Society could possibly carry out their duties in this respect with greater perseverance and courage as do these ignorant savages. The risks they will run, and the pluck they show in order to obtain and carry away their dead and wounded, is extraordinary, and shows what utter demoralisation they must have suffered on this occasion in order to leave so many bodies on the ground. Their losses were estimated, during the week's fighting, to be over two thousand, the greater part of which are reported to have been killed at Chakdara.

A good deal of rain fell while we were in camp at Amandara; but, in spite of this, the heat was still very trying to the troops. The 10th Field Battery, under Major Anderson, arrived at Khar on the 6th, having lost several horses from sunstroke on the march up. Several deaths also occurred at this time among our British troops, owing to the severe heat. But although the Swat Valley bears an evil reputation as regards climate at this time of the year, owing to malaria, which is bred of the swamps and rice-fields, yet we found it a pleasant enough change from the Malakand, where, perched high up among barren rocks, we received the full benefit of every storm which periodically swept these hills. Looking up the valley from Khar, the broad, rushing river, intersecting the green pastures of the valley, made a lovely foreground to the dark, rugged mountains which here enclose it. In places, immense quantities of long, silvery grass rose from the swamps on either side of the water, forming a curious contrast to the vivid green of the young rice-crops. Trees are scarce—in fact, the whole country is devoid of natural vegetation, and its people are too lazy or careless to plant fruit, such as apricot, pear or apple-trees, any of which would probably flourish—but vines are occasionally to be found, more especially in Upper Swat, where, on entering the small mud houses which constitute their villages, one frequently found oneself in an outer courtyard, enclosed on all sides by trellis work, from which the small green grapes hung in festoons.

Rumours were now brought in that the Bunerwals and Hindustani fanatics had started on the 5th to join the Upper Swatis in attacking us. Reconnaissances were therefore pushed some way up the valley, and every day the passes which lead into the Yuzafzai Plain were carefully watched by our cavalry. No enemy were to be found, however, much to the disappointment of the troops generally, who, having been shut up for over a week exposed to a hot fire by day and night, were now most eager to retaliate. Major Deane's news as to the Mad Mullah, in the meantime, showed that this fanatic was by no means idle. We heard that he was trying to raise the Shamozai villages against us on the night of the 5th, but receiving no encouragement here, he had moved to Abueh, and thence onward up the Swat Valley without obtaining a following. A few shots were fired at us occasionally during our reconnaissances by villagers and hillmen, but with no casualties on our side. The telegraph line between Chakdara and the Malakand, which had been completely destroyed by the tribesmen, who had carried away the wire and posts to their various homes, was now restored and put in working order, and a staging system of cart transport established from Nowshera for forwarding supplies. On the 8th August we received news of the attack on our fort at Shabkadr, near Peshawar, by the Mohmands—a tribe which we were eventually despatched to deal with. On the 11th, a rumour was received that a large jirgah or tribal council had been held by the Bunerwals with the Hindustani fanatics

THE SWAT VALLEY 87

and neighbouring tribes from Chamla, Khudukhel and Gadun, at which they had decided to join the Swatis, and had since left for Upper Swat; but, so far, no news of their arrival in that country had yet come in. The Lower Swatis, in the meantime, had submitted unconditionally, and were being allowed to return to their villages.

By the 14th August all transport arrangements for the force, detailed to march into Upper Swat with twelve days' supplies, were complete, and the force was ordered to concentrate at Thana the following day, the 11th Bengal Lancers, under Major Beatson, being sent on with orders to reconnoitre the country beyond so far as possible. Their information, derived from villagers, showed that many Bunerwals had crossed the passes from their country into Upper Swat; but although they had pushed on to a point whence they could see most of the country up to Landakai, a village in Upper Swat, they had not seen any signs of the enemy. Between Thana and Landakai, the only route possible lay through a narrow causeway about a mile in length, and barely broad enough to admit of one man passing along it at a time. This was flanked on one side by steep, rocky cliffs, the crests of which were strongly fortified by sungars, and on the other by the deep rapid torrent of the Swat River. Before reaching this causeway, a long ridge stretched from the hills to the small village of Jelala on our left. This was crowned by an ancient Buddhist fort, and several other ruins were scattered about on the neighbouring hills; the only relics of an ancient civilisation.

Owing to the bad weather, our advance was put off to the following day, on which the whole of the column marched to Thana. Rain fell in torrents all the morning, and our camp was a regular swamp. On arriving at Thana, Sir Bindon Blood heard that the enemy were occupying the causeway and ridge beyond Jelala. He at once rode out to reconnoitre, and on approaching Jelala, about four or five hundred of the enemy with fifteen standards were seen on the ridge, which they were evidently strengthening with sungars. Our appearance was greeted with a fusilade, and from their shouting defiance and light-hearted expenditure of ammunition, it was evident that larger numbers of them were in rear of their position. We returned to camp, which was well prepared for any attack they might make that night.

The tribesmen were, however, quite satisfied to stay where they were, and the narrow causeway, with an unfordable river on one side and high peaks on the other, was certainly the best strategical position they could have taken up, this being the door to the Upper Swat Valley, of which we were soon to produce the key which was destined to open it.

The next day, the 17th August, we were all on the move by daylight. All stores and baggage were packed up, and left in camp with the transport and followers, under charge of the baggage guards, strengthened by some additional troops to wait until the road in front should be cleared. At 6.30 the Guides Cavalry moved off under Colonel Adams, and pushing on to Jelala, found the enemy's advanced scouts and piquets established in the Buddhist ruins on the adjacent ridge. These they held in check, with the assistance of the advanced guard of the Royal West Kent, until the remainder of that battalion came up and cleared the position of the tribesmen, who fell back on their main body in rear. It was now seen that there were several thousands of the enemy occupying a front of some two miles along the heights in rear of this ridge, their right flank resting on the steep cliffs which commanded the causeway, their left reaching up to the higher hills which stretch away to the Morah Pass, and protected by an old Buddhist fort crowning one of the peaks. While the West Kent were en-

UPPER SWAT VALLEY

CALIFORNIA

gaged in clearing the first ridge, No. 7 British Mountain Battery, under Major Fegan, and No. 8 (Bengal) Mountain Battery, under Captain Birch, had formed up in rear of them, closely followed by the main body of the Infantry under Brigadier-General Meiklejohn. The 10th Field Battery had marched in rear of the column, lest it should find difficulty in passing along the road, which was very narrow in places, and thus cause delay to the troops.

But happily no such misfortune befel it, and after having negotiated some very difficult ground intersected by deep nullahs, Major Anderson brought it into action shortly before 9 A.M., opening fire from the ridge above Jelala, at a distance of 1600 yards, from where they did great execution among the crowd of Ghazis occupying a fort in the centre of their position. The effect of this fire, which was aided by Major Fegan's battery from a position higher up, was soon apparent: the enemy quickly evacuating the fort and sungars, and retiring under cover of the rocks and boulders to their rear, appearing now and again to fire at our infantry, whenever the fire from the batteries slackened. General Meiklejohn had meanwhile made a long flank march to envelop the enemy's left and sweep down the spur. This necessitated a long and arduous climb on the part of the 31st and 24th Punjab Infantry, who advanced to the assault, supported by No. 8 Mountain Battery and the 45th Sikhs.

These, on arriving at the objective point, caused considerable surprise to the enemy, who, as it was afterwards found out, had only looked for a frontal attack on the lower ground to the entrance of the causeway, and had in consequence posted considerable reserves in rear of their right flank to meet this contingency. This enveloping movement, therefore, caused great dismay; and the enemy, on seeing their line of retreat towards the Morah Pass threatened, broke up, a large portion of them streaming away to their left. The remainder, seeing that their force had been thus cut in half, soon lost heart; and after some desultory fighting, began to give way, falling back towards Landakai.

Prior to this, during an attempt on their part to reinforce their centre, a desperate charge of a handful of Ghazis took place. These fierce fanatics, preferring to die at the hands of the infidel and thus earn for themselves an immediate entrance into Paradise, rushed down the hill on to the bayonets of the 24th Punjab Infantry, there to meet the death they so eagerly sought.

The West Kent now commenced to clear the Landakai ridge and heights above the causeway, enabling the Sappers and Miners, under Captain Johnson, to repair the damages done to this narrow passage through which the cavalry were, in the meantime, anxiously awaiting their opportunity to advance; for it was thought probable that once through it, they would be able to catch the enemy retreating across the Landakai plain. At 11 A.M. the heights commanding the causeway were in the hands of our troops, and the Guides Cavalry commenced to file along this pass, every man being obliged to lead his horse until the open ground beyond was reached.

By the time that the head of the leading squadron had emerged into the plain, the enemy were already more than a mile away on the other side of it, and could be seen swarming up the hills in large numbers, many of them carrying standards of variegated colouring, red, green, and white being evidently the most popular tints. Owing to the constant rain of the preceding days, the ground had become exceedingly heavy, and being also cut up by several deep ravines, Captain Palmer, who had at once pushed forward in pursuit of a few tribesmen who had not yet reached the shelter of the hills, soon found himself far ahead of his men, who were unable to keep up with him. Near on his left was

Lieutenant R. T. Greaves, Lancashire Fusiliers, and behind him, at a distance of about thirty yards, rode Colonel Adams with his galloper, Lieutenant Norman, 11th Bengal Lancers; while at some distance, their men, consisting of about one troop in somewhat loose formation owing to the difficulties of the ground, followed as quickly as they could. After traversing a mile in this formation, some of the enemy were seen passing through a "ziarat" or graveyard, to a spur of a hill some eighty yards distant, from which the enemy were keeping up a fairly hot fire on our advancing men. Seeing that the enemy were in considerable force, Colonel Adams directed his men to the ziarat, intending, if possible, to hold that position until the infantry should arrive in support. Owing, however, to the noise of the firing, Palmer and Greaves were unable to hear him, and charged up to the foot of the hill, hoping to cut off a few tribesmen who were hastening towards it. The unfortunate occurrences of the next few minutes are best described by the following extract from a letter written by an officer who was present.

"On Palmer and Greaves approaching the hill, they were subjected to a heavy fire from the enemy. Palmer's horse was at once killed, while Greaves, having been shot at close quarters, fell, some twenty yards farther on, among the Pathans, who at once proceeded to hack at him with their swords. Seeing this, Adams and Fincastle went out to his assistance, followed by two sowars, who galloped towards Palmer, at that moment engaged in a hand-to-hand conflict with a standard-bearer. Palmer had been shot through the right wrist, and was only saved by the opportune appearance of these two men, who enabled him to get back to the shelter of the ziarat in safety. Meanwhile Fincastle, who had had his horse killed while galloping up to where Greaves lay, tried to lift Greaves on to Adams' horse, in the process of which Greaves was again shot through the body and Adams' horse wounded. They were soon joined by the two sowars who had been to Palmer's assistance, and almost immediately afterwards by Maclean, who, having first dismounted his squadron in the ziarat, had very pluckily ridden out, with four of his men, to the assistance of this small party, who otherwise would have been rushed by the enemy. With his assistance Greaves was successfully brought in, but unfortunately Maclean, who had dismounted in order to help in lifting the body on to his horse, was shot through both thighs, and died almost immediately."

It will be seen from the above extract that poor Maclean, who was quite the most popular officer in the force, was the means of saving the lives of the remainder of this small party. The scene of action took place at the foot of a hill with spurs jutting out on either side, from which the cross fire which the enemy poured in would have destroyed most of the squadron if Maclean had brought it out. With great judgment,

G

however, he had dismounted them in the ziarat, where they not only formed a support for the party to eventually retire on, but by their fire prevented the enemy from closing in and cutting them off, and then himself gallantly went to the assistance of his hard pressed comrades.

The loss of these two officers, both of whom were so deservedly popular, and held in high esteem both as soldiers and as friends, was one that appealed very directly to all the members of the force, and it was with hearts heavy with a sense of a personal misfortune that we continued the operations of the day.

The infantry and guns having now arrived on the scene, the enemy retired, falling back some two miles on the village of Abueh, where they came into collision with a squadron of the Guides under Captain Brazier Creagh, who soon dispersed them, the enemy taking refuge in the hills, where it was impossible to follow them up. Brazier Creagh thereupon returned to Kotah, having killed seven or eight of the enemy without any casualties on his side.

Meanwhile, our detachment left behind at Thana to guard the baggage and transport were not without occupation. During our advance on Jelala that morning, we had observed parties of the enemy moving along the high ridge leading from Landakai towards the Morah Pass. These men soon came in full view of our camp, and apparently imagined that it had been left unprotected, as about a thousand of them assembled, and with great shouting and beating of tom-toms began to descend the hills. As they showed considerable hesitation in committing themselves to the open, Colonel Bradshaw, 35th Sikhs, commanding the detachment in camp, sent Major Delamain, 11th Bengal Lancers, with two squadrons of his regiment to try and draw them on. They were too cautious, however, and the affair ended in a musketry engagement, in which Delamain inflicted a loss of twenty killed on the enemy, without any penalties on his own side, and ultimately caused them to retreat into Buner. After the conclusion of this action at Landakai, the 10th Field Battery, escorted by the two squadrons and some of the infantry, returned to Khar. The remainder of the force encamped on the plain near the village of Kotah, the fortifications of which were at once destroyed by the Sappers, and the fierceness of the flames from these towers, lighting up the dark gloom of the encircling hills, was all that remained to remind us of the day's events.

CHAPTER VII

MINGAORA—THE SACRED VILLAGE OF SAIDU — RECONNAISSANCE TO MINGLAOR — BUDDHIST RUINS

OUR losses during this action were very small, owing, no doubt, to the great use which was made of our artillery: eleven casualties on our side forming but a slight total against the heavy losses sustained by the enemy. General Wodehouse reported from Rustam that news had been received there that the Bunerwals, Gaduns, and Chagarzais, were streaming back to their villages, carrying numbers of their dead and wounded; while the Hindustani fanatics were said to have fled back to Kogah. The reports which gradually came in from the interior confirmed the decisive effect of this fight. The Mianguls sent in a letter the following day expressing general submission and a desire for peace; and from the information which we derived from the different villages we passed during the continuation of our march up the valley, there is no doubt that the Swatis suffered severely. The moral effect of our guns seems to have been very great, more especially that of the Field Battery, this being the first experience these tribesmen have had of this arm, an experience they will probably remember for some time to come.

We had now entered an unknown country: one which had not been penetrated by a white man since the days of Alexander the Great. For this reason the march up to Mingaora, although devoid of fighting, was full of interest; while the numerous Buddhist ruins, and mountain landscapes showing lofty snow-capped peaks in the distance, gave plenty of occupation to both the amateur archæologists and artists of our force. We arrived at Mingaora, which is the largest village in Upper Swat, on the 19th, and remained there, for a few days, while the country around was reconnoitred and surveyed.

The valley here widens to nearly four miles, covered with magnificent crops, and close to Mingaora lies the sacred village of Saidu, wherein lies the tomb of the famous Akhund of Swat, who, owing to his reputation for sanctity, obtained great influence over the tribes in Swat and neighbouring district. The Akhund died in the year 1877, and although his descendants, who are termed "Mianguls," have inherited his sanctity, they have very little authority compared to their predecessor. There are now four grandsons of the old patriarch alive, who, on our arrival at Mingaora, fled to the hills.

Owing to the village of Saidu being regarded as a sacred shrine, no one except Mohammedans were allowed to approach it, and we had to content ourselves with taking photographs of it from a distance. A few shots were fired into our camp on the first night of our arrival, but the headmen of the village having been told that they would be held responsible for any further occurrence of this sort, our remaining nights were undisturbed. A reconnaissance up the Swat Valley was carried out on the 21st, under Colonel Adams, during which we visited "Manglaor" or Mangla, as the old Buddhist records spell it. This is a good-sized village, and a great centre of commerce. We found in penetrating this upper portion of the Swat Valley that the only available route lay over the Shah-Melai Pass, about 4000 feet high, very steep, and covered with slippery rocks, over which we had great difficulty in dragging our horses.

The old Buddhist road, which, built some fifteen hundred years ago, stretches along the entire valley from the Malakand, here, curiously enough, runs along the bed of the valley, and on our arrival was covered with about three feet of water. During our stay at Mingaora, about eight hundred arms of all sorts were surrendered, among these being some of the rifles which had been taken during the attack on the Malakand.

Major Deane having finished his arrangements with the surrounding tribes, we marched back to Barikot on the 24th August, from where the next day a reconnaissance was pushed to the top of the Karakar Pass, leading into Buner. We found this pass entirely deserted by the enemy, who were occupied in watching General Wodehouse's force at Rustam, on the other side of the country, and except for a couple of scouts who fired off their rifles at us and decamped, we could have marched over this pass without opposition. Our route lay by a winding path up a deep ravine, fed by a stream of clear water, which intersected some lovely glades full of wild roses and jasmine, while higher up the hills became thickly wooded with pine-trees. Among the bare desolate mountains which surrounded us, this seemed indeed a little paradise, and one could have easily imagined oneself back in some quiet rustic spot in England.

The scene from the top of the pass, which is 3500 feet high, disclosed a panoramic view of the Amazai portion of Buner, and in the distance we could see the high mountains on the other side of the Indus. The country below us seemed to consist of broad and fertile valleys interspersed by low hills, which rose rather abruptly from the level, on which some large villages could be discerned. Fires were soon seen burning in various directions as signals of our presence, and a small gathering appeared as we were about to return to camp, but no hostilities were attempted during our descent.

We arrived back at the Malakand on the 27th of August, having now completely subdued the whole of the Swat Valley and adjacent tribes who had partaken in the recent rising, with the exception of the Bunerwals, who had received a severe punishment at our hands at Landakai, and who, it was expected, would give in to any terms our Government inflicted on them.

The Hindustani fanatics, who were reported as having taken part against us at Landakai, although now hardly to be regarded as a fighting force, were once a great factor for trouble on our frontier. Their history is a curious one, dating from about the year 1820, when a Mohammedan adventurer, "Saiad Ahmed Shah," having gained a great reputation for sanctity, and collected a large following of religious fanatics, established himself among the Yuzafzai tribes. Here, after many vicissitudes, he was finally slain in a battle against the Sikhs, and those of his following who escaped took up their abode on the Indus, beyond the Sikh frontier. Some time after, on our annexing the Peshawar district, they came into collision with our troops, and were driven out of this refuge.

These fanatics have always been a perpetual source of trouble to us. They were the cause of the Ambéla Campaign, at the close of which we drove them out of their settlement at Malka, owing to their continued depredations and outrages on our frontier; and their history since their expulsion from that district has been one of continued intrigue with the various tribes to obtain some convenient location for their colony, which has now dwindled down to about three hundred fighting men; and it is probable that the fierce fanaticism with which they do battle on every occasion they meet us will do much to diminish their number. Although they follow the Mohammedan religion, their creed is very unorthodox, being similar to that of the Wahabi sect; and during the jehad or religious war, which was preached against us by the Mullahs previous to the rising along the frontier this year (1897), it was a matter of speculation to see if it developed into a Wahabi movement, in which case large numbers of recruits would have joined this sect from all parts of India. This was not the case, however, and there is no doubt that their power is diminishing rapidly, owing to the few recruits they have received of late years. It certainly

UNIV. OF
CALIFORNIA

BUDDHIST STUPA, SHANKARGHAR

requires an extraordinary amount of religious enthusiasm to enable these people to leave their homes in India and take up their abode among savage hill tribes in some of the most inhospitable regions in the world.

Among the numerous relics of Buddhism, which were the chief characteristics of the Swat Valley, one which interested us greatly was a large "stupa" or "tope" near the village of Shankarghar in Upper Swat. This stupa was a conical mass of masonry with a flat circular surface above and a small chamber in its base, which was almost completely enveloped in a heap of rubbish and stones. In these rubbish heaps, coins and fragments of idols are usually found in large quantities. These relics date from the Buddhist era about 250 B.C. Nearly all the ancient ruins in these districts are of Buddhist origin; some of even more ancient date, reaching back to the time of Alexander the Great, who, advancing on India from Cabul, divided his force into two divisions, one of which he marched through Bajour, Swat and Buner, crossing the Indus into the Yuzafzai plain, while the other proceeded to the same river by a more direct route. From the accounts given of Alexander's progress through these districts, which were then peopled by Indian tribes, his troops must have fought many pitched battles, and it is probable that the country at that time possessed a far larger and more prosperous population, from the appearance of the ruins of the large fortified cities which can still be traced, while the soil must have been very fertile to support the huge army which marched through it. Alexander died in 323 B.C., and it was shortly after this date that Buddhism established itself among these mountainous districts, which have never since enjoyed such a flourishing civilisation.

CHAPTER VIII

EXPEDITION AGAINST THE MOHMANDS — SEIZURE OF THE PANJKORA BRIDGE — MARCH THROUGH BAJOUR — NIGHT ATTACK ON SECOND BRIGADE

ON the 27th August, Sir Bindon Blood moved his headquarters to Malakand, and on the 28th orders were issued for an advance into the Utman Khel country. Brigadier-General Jeffreys with the Second Brigade was accordingly ordered to move down from Khar to Jolagram, and from thence down to the Utman Khel country, coming out at the south-west end near Abazai; while, at the same time, a force under Colonel Reid was ordered to concentrate at Uch, about seven miles north of Chakdara, in order to support the Nawab of Dir, who was dealing with those villages in his own territory who had been implicated in the recent rising.

General Jeffreys started off his brigade to Jolagram on the 28th, and, although delayed by very heavy rain, managed to march down the river to Kalangai on the 30th. The first part of the road lay over a rocky spur which ran down to the Swat River, which necessitated some hard work for the Sappers before it was made fit for the passage of our troops. After passing this spur, the road emerges into the Matkanai Valley, where the scenery is very striking, lofty hills clad with pines surround the valley, and picturesque groups of old Buddhist ruins stand out on every spur and salient point. In one "ziarat" or graveyard, we found even the tombstones made out of fragments of Buddhist sculpture.

On arrival at Kalangai, the Sappers, escorted by the Guides Infantry, were sent off to reconnoitre the Inziri Pass and improve the road; but, on return to camp in the evening, we heard that a message

KOH-I-MOHR, IN THE BAJAUR VALLEY

had just been received from Sir Bindon Blood that the brigade was to march back to Khar the next day. We accordingly went back, and halted at Khar till the 6th September.

Meanwhile, General Wodehouse had marched his brigade up from Rustam, and thus there were three brigades mobilised within reach of the Malakand. On the 6th, orders were received to march two brigades through Bajour and the Mohmand country, to emerge finally at Shabkadr, near Peshawar, co-operating with a force which, under Major-General Elles, C.B., was to move north through the Mohmand country from Shabkadr.

In anticipation of a move in this direction, a force had already been despatched under General Wodehouse to seize the bridge over the Panjkora, which was accomplished on the 4th September; and from information received by Major Deane shortly afterwards, this strategical move on our part only anticipated the tribesmen on the other side of the river by a few hours. The 10th Field Battery accompanied General Wodehouse's brigade, a creditable performance, considering the narrow mountain track which constituted the only available route to the river. The Artillery driving competition at the Agricultural Hall could hardly compete with this feat, where the least mistake on the part of the drivers or horses would mean probably a whole gun-team and gun falling over a precipice into the river below.

General Meiklejohn, having assumed command of the line of communication, the Second Brigade left Khar on the 6th, and marched up one day in rear of the Third Brigade, which, accompanied by Sir Bindon Blood, crossed the Panjkora without opposition on the 8th, and marched up the Nawagai Valley. On our way through Bajour we halted at Ghosam, a name familiar to many who took part in the Chitral campaign, as it is within a mile of Mundah, in the Jandol Valley, which was one of the largest posts on the line to Chitral, and the entrenchments of the old camp and even traces of the old huts and shelters were still visible. From Ghosam, Major Deane settled with the various villages who had taken part in the attack on Chakdara.

Amongst these were the villages belonging to two of Umra Khan's brothers, Mir Hassan Khan and Mir Afzal Khan, who were re-established by us in the Jandol Valley in 1895, after the Chitral expedition, and who had since taken part against us by forcing the Panjkora bridge, held at the time by the Khan of Dir's men, thus enabling the tribesmen from the far side of the Panjkora river to join in the attacks on Malakand and Chakdara. As a punishment for this, they were ordered to surrender a certain number of rifles, which were at once handed in.

During a reconnaissance up the Jandol Valley, we paid a visit to Barwa Fort, formerly the headquarters of Umra Khan, but now held by a cousin of his, Said Ahmed Khan, who entertained us in the most hospitable manner. It was in this fort that Lieutenants Edwards and Fowler were imprisoned by Umra Khan in 1895. The character of the tribes up here is well shown by the numerous forts with which every valley is filled. The inhabitants build their mud houses within a defensive loop-holed wall, containing but one entrance with a strong tower at each corner, and from these strongholds carry on perpetual feuds with their neighbours. In fact, the normal condition of these people is one of continual war and bloodshed.

It was still very hot here during the day, but the nights were rapidly getting cooler, and the health of the troops was excellent; while as for our transport animals, out of over two thousand mules belonging to the Second Brigade, only seventeen were reported unfit for work at Ghosam. During our halt here, the Khan of Nawagai, who is by far the largest landowner and most powerful chief in Bajour, sent in a letter to Major Deane to say that he and Khans of Khar,*

* The one being his brother, the other his cousin.

THE MOHMANDS

and Jhar, would assist us as far as they were able in our march through their territory. This promise was afterwards fully carried out; and in spite of the pressure brought to bear on them by their own people and the surrounding tribes, these Khans remained loyal to us throughout our stay in these regions.

From Shamshak, on the 13th September, Sir Bindon Blood reconnoitred the Rambat Pass which leads out of the Nawagai Valley into the Mohmand district, and finding that the country to the south of it, through which our troops would have to march, was very deficient in water and forage, he directed General Jeffreys to cross it on the 15th, taking two battalions, a company of Sappers, and one squadron of cavalry, with five days' supplies for the force; sending the remainder of his troops to join the Third Brigade at Nawagai, to which place he, Sir Bindon, marched on the 14th.

The idea was that these two brigades should cut off all communications with the

Malakand, cross into the Mohmand country by the Rambat Pass and Nawagai, and carrying rations up to the 22nd, march south through the Mohmand country until communication was effected with General Elles' force, which was to leave Shabkadr on the 15th.

Accordingly, on the 14th, the Third Brigade marched to Nawagai, while General Jeffreys encamped at a place called Markhanai, near the foot of the Rambat Pass. Part of the Second Brigade, consisting of the Buffs and 4th Company Bengal Sappers and Miners, were detached by General Jeffreys to the crest of the Rambat Pass to prepare the road for the passage of his force next morning, and to bivouac there for the night. The road up to the pass was partially made, and next day the brigade would have marched over; but the best plans are sometimes upset by some unforeseen occurrence, and in this case a night attack changed the whole aspect of affairs. The ground about Markhanai was much intersected with deep precipitous ravines, and the camp was situated on the edge of one of these, whilst on the other side was a dip of the ground capable of affording cover from our fire. About 8 P.M. the camp was suddenly assailed by a heavy musketry fire from the deep ravine, a veritable storm of bullets sweeping the camp. All lights were immediately extinguished, and the men fell in rapidly and silently on the trenches opening fire on our unseen foe, who had gradually moved round to the other side of the camp. It was pitch dark, as the moon had not yet risen; and the enemy, emboldened by this, could be heard shouting and beating tom-toms in close proximity. But, in spite of star shells being fired by Captain Birch's battery, very few of them were seen, and they never attempted to rush the camp, being contented with pouring in a murderous fire, which, as they were armed mostly with rifles, soon caused many casualties, these being chiefly amongst the horses and transport mules. Every few minutes the "thud" of a bullet would be heard, on which some wretched animal would rear up and fall over in its death struggle.

The fire was hottest on the side occupied by the 38th Dogras, and it was determined to make a sortie to try and clear the enemy out of the numerous small ravines on that flank. The bullets were sweeping the ground in such a manner that to stand up meant almost certain death, in spite of which several men volunteered for the sortie.

Captain Tomkins, 38th Dogras, was at once shot dead before the start, and Lieutenant Bailey of the same regiment fell almost simultaneously; Lieutenant Harrington, 26th Punjab Infantry, who was at that time attached to the Dogras, was shot through the head, from the effects of which wound he afterwards died at Panjkora.

Several men were also killed and wounded

at this juncture; in fact, the enemy's fire was so hot that it was found impossible to carry out the sortie, more especially as the moon had just risen, and anyone standing up stood out in silhouette against its light. The attack died away about 11.30 P.M., and we could hear the enemy moving off and shouting in the distance, as they went towards the Nawagai stream, where they lit several bonfires.

All was quiet till about 1 A.M., when they again came on and kept up a hot fire until 3 A.M., without a break, never attempting, however, to rush the camp. Among them was a bugler, who was most energetic in his musical efforts the whole night; while another man sat in the deep nullah on one side of the camp, and shouted out directions to his brethren on the other side. He was probably their instructor of musketry, as he kept on yelling, "Shoot low, shoot low, all your bullets are going high; kill the pigs, kill them!" He had hidden himself so effectually that, although we fired many shots at him, it is probable that he escaped untouched.

Next morning the camp was a sad sight, dead horses and mules lying all over the place, among the tents and shelters which had been hurriedly thrown down during the night, and everyone was mourning the sad loss of our brother officers and men who had been killed in such unsatisfactory warfare.

A SIKH ORDERLY

CHAPTER IX

PURSUIT OF THE ENEMY — INAYAT KILA — MARCH UP THE MAMUND VALLEY — SEVERE FIGHTING — DIFFICULTIES OF RETIREMENT

HAVING ascertained that the men who had attacked us were a section of the Bajour tribes living in the Mamund Valley, General Jeffreys at once despatched a squadron of the 11th Bengal Lancers, under Captain Cole, in pursuit.

By dint of hard riding, Cole caught the enemy near the village of Inayat Kila, at the entrance to their valley, killing many of them, and pursuing the remainder some four or five miles before he was obliged to retire on Inayat Kila, where he was joined by the Guides Infantry, under Major Campbell, and Captain Birch's Mountain

Battery, which had been sent out in support. This was, however, too small a force to follow up the enemy among the intricate defiles of their rugged and precipitous hills; so, while the Guides, supported by the guns, destroyed the fortifications of several small villages in the vicinity without opposition, a camping-ground was selected near Inayat Kila, a message having been received from General Jeffreys, stating that he would shortly arrive with the rest of the brigade. This camping-ground was chosen by Major Campbell, about a mile south of Inayat Kila, on an open plain, well away from any nullahs which might give cover to the enemy at night, and the remainder of the brigade, including the Buffs and the Sappers, who had been recalled from the Rambat Pass, arrived in the course of the afternoon. The camp was at once entrenched, and every precaution taken against another attack, and the night passed without a single shot being fired.

MAMUND VALLEY

The following day, the 16th September, was to witness some of the hardest fighting which we had yet experienced. Long before dawn, the bustle and noise of men moving about and preparing their coffee announced an early start, and shortly after *reveille* had been sounded, the troops fell in preparatory to marching. The force was divided into three columns: the right column, consisting of six companies 38th Dogras and a detachment of Sappers under Colonel Vivian, was directed to cross the Watelai stream, and proceed against certain Mamund villages on the eastern side of the valley; while on the left, Major Campbell of the Guides, with five companies of his regiment and two of the Buffs, had orders to operate against several villages on the western side of the valley, keeping touch with the centre column, which consisted of four companies of the Buffs, six companies of the 35th Sikhs, four guns of the Peshawar Mountain Battery, and a squadron of cavalry, the whole under command of Colonel Goldney, who had been directed to move straight up the valley.

Colonel Vivian with the left column, after having successfully captured several small villages, found himself checked by a large force of the enemy, who held too strong a position for him to attack with the force at his disposal. He therefore returned to camp, arriving there at 4 P.M., having had two men wounded during the day.

The centre column meanwhile advanced some six miles up the valley without opposition, the enemy being first reported at Badam Kila, to which place a detachment of the Buffs under Colonel Ommaney was sent to dislodge them. The remainder of the column pushed on, and about 10.30 A.M. the two companies of the 35th Sikhs leading the advance had occupied a knoll above the village of "Shahi Tangi," which was the farthest point reached by the brigade that day, being upwards of nine miles from camp. These two companies, while advancing on Shahi Tangi, got somewhat too far ahead of their support, and were attacked by the enemy in such large numbers that they were forced to retire about a mile. This movement was carried out under great difficulties. Hampered by their wounded, many of our men were unable to return the fire of the tribesmen, who swarmed round, pouring in a heavy and disastrous fire at close quarters.

Their difficulties increased at every step, as the Ghazis, seeing their opportunity, pressed ever closer, their swordsmen charging in and cutting down the Sikhs in the ranks, seventeen being thus killed or wounded. Soon they were unable to carry their comrades, so depleted were their ranks; and Lieutenant Hughes, the adjutant of the regiment, being shot through the body, was among those left on the ground, shortly to be recovered, however, by his men and the Buffs who arrived in support.

Just as this reinforcement took place, a squadron of the 11th Bengal Lancers under Cole dashed out, and the brilliant and opportune charge of this small handful of cavalry effectually routed the Ghazis, many of whom were speared before they could reach the shelter of the adjacent hills. From this refuge they were then ousted by the Buffs, who, driving the enemy before them, soon regained all the lost ground, the tribesmen, in their flight, leaving many dead and wounded behind them.

Meanwhile the left column, under Major Campbell, had remained on the western side of the valley some considerable distance behind, being fully occupied in destroying the defences of the numerous villages met with shortly after leaving camp. About 9 A.M. Major Campbell received a helio message from General Jeffreys to come up as soon as possible and support the Buffs and 35th Sikhs, as the enemy were appearing in large numbers from the direction of the villages of Agrah and Gat, on the northern slope of the valley. Campbell immediately collected all his companies and started off, joining the centre column about noon. Taking up a position on their left flank along the edge of a broad ravine, that officer kept over a thousand of the enemy in check. Many of these were dressed in khaki closely resembling, in the distance, the uniform of our soldiers, and were said to be Umra Khan's men, who had their headquarters in the neighbouring village of Zagai.

Captain Birch's battery was fully occupied all this time. When the Buffs arrived in support of the 35th Sikhs, and stormed the hill to recover the position which the two companies of Sikhs had been forced to abandon, Birch brought his guns into action above Chingai, from where he was able to do great execution among the flying tribesmen. To this position Captain Ryder and Lieutenant Gunning, with one and a half companies of the 35th Sikhs, were sent to hold the high hill on the right of the guns, and, owing to subsequent orders not reaching them, advanced up the hill farther than was originally intended.

This was shortly afterwards realised, when, at 3 P.M., General Jeffreys ordered the troops to return to camp; for the ridge which Ryder and his small party of Sikhs had occupied, and along which they now commenced to retire, slightly diverged from the line of march which the main body in their return to camp were following. Ryder soon found himself in an awkward position: isolated from the remainder of the force; hard pressed by the tribesmen; hampered by the wounded, and running short of ammunition, he was soon obliged to send an urgent appeal for help.

On receipt of this message, General Jeffreys ordered the Guides under Major Campbell to go to Ryder's assistance; but already, before Campbell received these orders, half a company of Guides, who were with the reserve ammunition, had been sent off under a native officer to try and join Ryder's party, who were some fifteen hundred feet above us. As Ryder's party was, moreover, completely out of sight, bugles were sounded to try and obtain information as to their whereabouts, while the Guides moved off to the right flank. Surgeon-Lieutenant Fisher had already made a gallant attempt to reach Ryder with some dhoolies to carry away the wounded, but, finding it impossible to get his dhoolies up the precipitous hillside, had been obliged to return.

A little while later and Ryder, with his Sikhs, could be seen fighting their way step by step down a steep rocky spur south of the village of Badelai, assisted by the half-company of Guides, who had fortunately been able to reach them with a small supply of ammunition. Still the position of this force was an extremely critical one, for the tribesmen, confident that they had cut off this small band from all outside help, now rushed in with their swords, trying to overcome by force of numbers the steady resistance offered them. Both Ryder and Gunning had been wounded; the latter very severely, being shot in both the face and the shoulder, besides having received two deep sword-cuts on the back. Fortunately Campbell, with the remainder of the Guides, soon arrived at the foot of the hill, from where he was able to deliver several volleys into the midst of the enemy, which checked their farther advance. Ali Gul, an Afridi havildar of the Guides, then volunteered to go up the hill with ammunition for the Sikhs, whose supply had run short.

Taking as many packets as he could carry, he climbed up the hill, distributed the cartridges, and carried back a wounded subadar of the Sikhs; an example which was quickly followed by his comrades in the Guides, who swarmed up the hill to help in carrying back the wounded Sikhs.

By the time they had all reached the valley below, evening was closing in, and the main body were at some distance on their return march to camp; favoured by the gathering gloom, the Ghazis closed in on all sides, creeping up the ravines and pouring in a hot fire at close quarters on the

Guides, who, with the Sikhs and numerous wounded of Ryder's party, followed the same route as the main body.

It soon became pitch dark, and the difficulties of the march were much increased by a heavy storm which now burst. Amidst the thunder and rain and the blackness of the night, this force lost the line of retreat followed by the remainder of the brigade, and but for the vivid lightning which continuously lit up the scene, would have found it almost impossible to have made their way across the deep ravines which cut up the valley in all directions.

It was 10 P.M. when they reached the camp at Inayat Kila, amidst a deluge of rain, which had converted every small nullah into a roaring torrent. Here they found that General Jeffreys, with part of his brigade, had not yet returned.* Two companies of the Guides had already been despatched to his assistance; for the remainder of the

---

* These two companies had been in camp all day.

force there was nothing now to be done on such a night but await with anxiety for the dawn, officers and men lying down as they were, wet through and exhausted with the hard work of the day.

CHAPTER X

GENERAL JEFFREYS BENIGHTED—VILLAGE OF BILOT—HEAVY THUNDERSTORM—LOSSES IN THE MOUNTAIN BATTERY—PUNITIVE OPERATIONS

DAWN at last appeared, and with it General Jeffreys and the Mountain Battery,* which, with a section of Sappers and twelve men of the Buffs, had got separated from the remainder of the Brigade during the homeward march on the previous evening. Benighted, in a country cut up by deep ravines, General Jeffreys had decided to bivouac where he was until daylight, and for this purpose selected a village,† which had been previously set fire to by our troops, part of it being still in

---

* Four guns No. 8 British Mountain Battery, commanded by Captain Birch, R.A.
† Village of Bilot.

flames. Shortly before this village was reached, four companies * under Major Worledge arrived, but these were at once sent off to the support of the Guides, and the guns, with their small escort, took up their position in a re-entering angle formed by the walls of this village. Defences were at once formed, but most of the mules, with the entrenching tools, having gone on to camp, the Sappers were obliged to use their bayonets in order to throw up the rough and hasty shelter trench which protected one side, while on the other the gunners proceeded to make a parapet to protect their guns. Luckily the ground was soft, and the defences thus hurriedly organised were beginning to take shape when some of the enemy got possession of the unoccupied portion of the village, and commenced firing on our troops. Although the strength of the enemy was unknown,

---

* Two companies 35th Sikhs, and two companies Guides Infantry. These had been ordered out from the camp, which Major Worledge had been left in charge of for that day.

and there were but few men available, a gallant attempt was made to turn them out by Lieutenant Watson, R.E., who soon returned, shot through the leg. Although wounded, Watson made another attempt. This was also unavailing, and, being now badly wounded in both arms, and with two of his men hit, he was obliged to give it up.

The fire which the enemy brought to bear was so hot that it appeared absolutely necessary, however, to clear the village; so in spite of the failure of the former attempts, Lieutenant Colvin, R.E., taking eight Sappers with him, being unable to take more for fear of weakening the gun's escort, made a dash into the village, through a doorway in the wall, and climbing up on to the roof of a small house, fired into the enemy below. As there proved to be men all round them, the position soon became untenable: in fact, it was apparent that the village was a regular maze, and being absolutely unknown to our men, it was evidently impossible to clear the place without reinforcements.

By this time the enemy had adopted bolder tactics, trying to rush our troops over the shelter trench, while others fired over the wall into the small space where men and mules were packed together. Casualties increased. General Jeffreys, amongst others, was wounded, receiving a severe cut on the head from a rock thrown down from above by one of the Mamunds.

The left flank of the shelter trench was now thrown back, owing to that part near the wall being enfiladed, and the men, while throwing up this fresh defensive work, being forced to fix bayonets lest they should be rushed by the enemy, were obliged to use their hands. Saddles were taken off the mules, and these and the ammunition boxes were the only cover available for this small force, many of whom by now had been killed or wounded.

About 9 P.M. it began to rain, this being the first symptoms of the severe thunderstorm which shortly afterwards broke. The fury with which this storm raged probably saved many casualties on our side, while the rain proved a great boon to the wounded, for whom there was no water available otherwise. The situation was rapidly becoming critical as our men dropped, many of them still continuing to serve the guns and man the shelter trench in spite of their wounds, among these being Lieutenant Wynter, who, shot through both legs, remained at his post until, through faintness from loss of blood, he could no longer give orders.

About midnight, when the storm had ceased and the moon was beginning to rise, a sowar rode in, having been sent out by Major Worledge to find General Jeffreys' position. It appeared that, failing to find the Guides whom he had been previously sent out to support, Major Worledge had attempted to retrace his steps and rejoin the General, but, owing to the storm, had failed to find him, and had halted for some time close to Bilot, unaware of the critical position of the General within a short distance of him. The storm abating, however, the sound of the guns could be heard, and a sowar was at once despatched to find out the General's exact position. All anxiety was now over, for, reinforced by these four companies, the enemy were cleared out of the village, and the troops remained undisturbed until daybreak, when they proceeded to march home.

Ankle-deep in mud, the sodden tents looking limp and dejected in the grey of the morning, many of them knocked over by the storm of the previous night, the camp was anything but cheerful that morning; and never was sun more welcome than when it topped the surrounding hills, and sent its warm rays to dry the shivering garrison, while the missing troops marched in, footsore and weary, bearing a very different aspect to the men who had marched out to meet the enemy but twenty-four hours before. The roll-call of the various regiments now showed us the full extent of our losses. These were fairly heavy; two officers and thirty-six men having been killed, while the wounded numbered five officers and one hundred and two men. The mountain battery had fared badly, having lost an officer and six men killed with twenty-two wounded, besides having thirty-one mules killed.

The following are the names of British officers killed and wounded in this action:—

KILLED

Lieutenant A. T. Crawford, Royal Artillery.
Lieutenant V. Hughes, 35th Sikhs.

WOUNDED

Captain W. J. Ryder, attached 35th Sikhs.
Lieutenant O. G. Gunning, 35th Sikhs.
Lieutenant G. R. Cassels, 35th Sikhs.
Lieutenant T. C. Watson, Royal Engineers.
Lieutenant F. A. Wynter, Royal Artillery.

Next day, the 18th September, saw us once more on our way up the valley, to punish the Mamunds. Marching out early in the morning, we proceeded to attack

"Damadolah," a strongly-fortified village on the eastern side of the valley, some six miles distant from the camp.

The valley looked wonderfully green and fresh after its recent shower of rain, even the bleak Afghan hills had donned a new garment of variegated colours. Damadolah lay at the foot of one of these hills, surrounded by crops of millet and Indian corn, through which we could see the flash of the enemy's sword-blades, as, summoned by the sound of the tom-tom, parties of them hastened from all parts of the valley to the support of their comrades. We had been obliged to follow a winding path, along a deep ravine, and had only debouched into the open, about two thousand yards from the enemy's position, our appearance being the signal for the enemy to "fall in," and as we advanced we could see them making their dispositions to meet our attack.

No time was lost. The 35th Sikhs and 38th Dogras, with the Buffs in support,

A MALIK IN THE MANU'ND VALLEY

CALIFORNIA

stormed the heights on either flank, the tribesmen making no attempt to stand, while the Guides advanced straight on the village, which was captured and destroyed without any loss on our side. The enemy retired to the heights above, and kept up a desultory fire, checked in all their attempts to collect in any force by the fire of the mountain battery, which commanded the whole face of the hill. Our transport having loaded up with the captured grain, we returned to camp, followed up by the enemy, who, however, never succeeded in getting to close quarters. Our casualties during the whole day were two killed and six wounded.

On the 19th a foraging party was sent to collect grain from a village some three miles from camp. Large quantities of grain were found, mostly buried underground, but owing to the fresh appearance of the flattened soil, we were able to discover these hiding-places without much difficulty. The tribesmen made no attempt to engage us, owing to the village being situated in the open valley, close to our camp.

The following day the whole brigade was ordered out, the intention being to attack Umra Khan's village, Zagai, which stood at the head of the valley, some seven or eight miles distant.

Attacking a village in the Mamund Valley had for all of us by now a monotony which was only varied according to the amount of opposition offered, and to the losses we suffered. Every attack took place under almost similar circumstances. On nearing the village, the tribesmen would beat their tom-toms, and thus summon their comrades from all parts of the valley; white and green standards, bearing the strange and weird device of a blood-red hand, would be seen heading parties of hurrying Ghazis, eager for the coming combat; their curved swords glistening in the bright sunlight, the swordsmen would gather on the tops of the hills, ready for their downward rush, while behind every rock and stone crouched a Ghazi, rifle in hand, awaiting our arrival.

There was but little variation this time. On nearing the foot of the hill we found the village, as usual, occupying a strong position, protected by the overhanging cliffs and steep, ragged spurs which ran down on either side of it. These spurs were told off to the Guides Infantry and the Buffs, while the 38th Dogras advanced straight on the village,—the 35th Sikhs being held in reserve.

The Guides gained possession of their spur without much difficulty, but on the right the Buffs met with some opposition from the tribesmen, who poured in a hot fire on our advancing troops. The Buffs, however, drove all before them in their steady and determined advance. Eleven casualties occurred in as many seconds, among these being two of their officers, Lieutenants Keene and Power, both of whom were severely wounded.

The heights on either side being captured, the Dogras rushed the village, and in a few minutes fortifications and towers were seen hurtling through the air, while, from the hills around, came the echo of the explosion.

While the defences were thus being destroyed, many of the enemy were seen collecting on the other side of the valley. These threatened to work round our left flank, but the appearance of a squadron of the 11th Bengal Lancers soon checked them. The tribesmen, always in terror lest they should be caught in the open by the cavalry, were thus practically kept *hors de combat* for the remainder of the day, and, our operations completed, we returned to camp without further casualties.

CHAPTER XI

POSITION OF FIRST BRIGADE AT NAWAGAI — THE HADDA MULLAH — TWO NIGHT ATTACKS — GENERAL WODEHOUSE WOUNDED

MEANWHILE the Third Brigade were camped at Nawagai, having crossed a watershed at the end of the Watelai Valley and taken up a position on the plain which stretches from the small village and fort of Nawagai to the hills around the Bedmanai Pass, where the Hadda Mullah was reported to have collected his forces. Owing to the night attack of the 15th, with the consequent turning aside of General Jeffreys' brigade, a considerable change in plans was now necessary, and Sir Bindon Blood determined to stay where he was, until the arrival of General Elles' force should enable him to attack the Hadda Mullah in his stronghold in the hills, and clear out the Bedmanai Pass and neighbouring valleys with completeness.

Great pressure was being put on the Khan of Nawagai at this time, both by the neighbouring tribes and by his own people, in order to induce him to withdraw from his support of our troops; and there is small doubt that if it had not been for the presence of the Third Brigade at Nawagai, the Khan would either have been obliged to join the hostile tribes, or would have been forced to fly from the valley, in which case the whole of his people, consisting of the most numerous and best-armed portion of Bajour, would have risen against us. Not only would we thus have had an enormous force to contend with, but there would also have been great danger of the movement spreading up to Dir and Chitral, for although the Nawab of Dir had hitherto been able to assert his authority, it is certain that, in the case of a combined tribal movement, no reliance could be placed on his levies, and neither he nor the Khan of Nawagai would be strong enough to stem the rising tide of fanaticism.

The strategical importance of the position of the Third Brigade at Nawagai was therefore immense, as it divided the two hostile forces, the Hadda Mullah's and the Mamunds, and prevented the remainder of the country joining them: although, with hostile tribes in rear, and the possibility of the Nawagai people rising in arms against us, the force was not strong enough to attack the Hadda Mullah in his stronghold in the Bedmanai Pass, a defile some seven or eight miles long. For if the Brigade had moved forward against the Hadda Mullah's tribesmen, a considerable force must have been left behind to guard the camp, which from a strength of only three battalions could not have been spared.

To the foot of the high hills which rose on either side of the Bedmanai Pass some seven miles from our camp, the intervening ground was a flat, waterless plain, favourable for cavalry, until close under the hills, where the ground became deeply cut up by ravines. Our camp was situated within reach of a stream which ran through the village of Nawagai, from which we were distant about one mile. A few days were spent in reconnoitring the country; the cavalry penetrating some twenty-two miles to Ato Khel, a village a few miles north of the Nahaki (or Nakki) Pass, over which General Elles was daily expected. The reconnaissance, which was made by Major Beatson and Captain Stanton* with one squadron of the 11th Bengal Lancers, obtained no news, however, of General Elles' force, and it was evident that he had been delayed by the difficulties of the route. The Hadda Mullah's gathering was meanwhile reported to be daily increasing in numbers, and whenever our patrols approached the hills, they were fired on by small parties and scouts of the enemy.

* D.A.Q.M.G. for intelligence.

Our first meeting with the enemy in force occurred on the afternoon of the 17th. We saw about fifteen hundred of the Hadda Mullah's clansmen apparently advancing on our camp, when the brigade was at once turned out; but as the enemy, on seeing us, remained close under the hills, with a network of ravines between our two forces, we were unable to come to close quarters owing to approaching night. A few shots were exchanged, and our Mountain Battery dropped a shell or two amongst them, after which we returned home lest we should be benighted; a prospect which meant our having to fight our way back to camp through several ravines, with every advantage on the side of the enemy.

The next day heliographic communication was opened with General Elles' force, which had arrived on the top of the Nahaki Pass, and on the following day instructions, through this means, were received stating that we were to join General

Jeffreys in the Mamund Valley. It was not practicable, however, to carry out these instructions until General Elles should arrive on the Nawagai Plain to protect the Khan of Nawagai from the Hadda Mullah's force, which was now reported to number over four thousand men. During our stay here "snipers" and small parties of the enemy hung about our camp on the lookout to cut up any stray members of our force; but hitherto no soldiers or followers had lost their lives, owing to the strict regulations that were enforced to prevent straggling on the march and straying from camp. That morning, however, a private of the Queen's West Surrey Regiment was stabbed to death while standing within three yards of his piquet. So sudden was the rush of the three men who crept up in the dark to commit this deed, that they had disappeared under cover of the network of deep ravines that surrounded the camp before the piquet had time to fire.

About five in the evening, the enemy again appeared in the plain, at the mouth of the Bedmanai Pass. We turned out, more to have a look at them than anything else, as it was too late to engage them at such a distance from camp. There appeared to be from two to three thousand of them, who, on our appearance, fired off their jezails and guns in the air, shouting and dancing, presumably to show their defiance, keeping at some distance from us, however, until we retired, when they advanced, following us up to camp, and the Khan of Nawagai's son informed us that they meant to attack before morning.

All seemed quiet that night until at 11 P.M. a couple of hundred swordsmen, having crept up a ravine to within fifty yards of our camp, suddenly charged that portion of it which was defended by the 1st Battalion Queen's West Surrey Regiment. They were met by such a hail of bullets that most of them stopped, and of the remainder not a man reached our line alive.

The main body of the enemy were meanwhile in reserve, waiting for their opportunity to follow up the rush of their first party if they should succeed in penetrating our lines, but finding their first effort so easily repulsed, they attempted to rush other parts of the camp, only in a half-hearted way, withdrawing soon after to engage the Khan of Nawagai's men, who were on outpost duty about a mile distant. This they evidently found more congenial work as a brisk skirmish ensued, which finally ended in the enemy's disappearance soon after midnight. Our casualties in this skirmish were one British soldier killed and one severely wounded. Several horses and transport animals were killed and disabled.

The next day Sir Bindon Blood received a message from General Elles, asking him to meet him on the 21st at Lakerai, about ten miles distant, to which place he would march with his First Brigade. This was good news, as Sir Bindon, who was anxious to return to the Mamund Valley, where the opposition seemed likely to be severe, would now be able to leave Nawagai on the following day. That afternoon, news having been brought in that a large contingent of Shinwarris, under the Suffi Mullah, had arrived in the Bedmanai Pass to reinforce the Hadda Mullah's gathering, a reconnaissance in force was made to the mouth of the pass. The enemy showed themselves in considerable force, but were evidently averse to coming within effective range of our guns, but during our return to camp they followed us up, as on the previous occasion, keeping well under the the hills, lest we should catch them on the open plain, and when last seen, just before darkness set in, they were only two miles from camp. They were in large numbers, afterwards estimated from the information brought in at five thousand men, and they had evidently been worked up to the highest pitch of fanaticism by the way they advanced over the plain, beating tom-toms, yelling and dancing a wild Khattak dance, with a vast expenditure of ammunition.

After these warlike demonstrations, we were not surprised when, at about 9 P.M., the enemy who had crept silently up the deep nullahs around the camp, attempted to rush us simultaneously from three sides. We were well prepared, but, owing to the pitch darkness, the first few minutes were rather warm work, as the enemy's swordsmen simply hurled themselves against our entrenchments, utterly regardless of their losses; and if they had once succeeded in forcing an entrance, the large numbers with which they would at once have poured in, together with the confusion consequent on the darkness, must at least have resulted in heavy losses to the defenders. As it was, the steadiness of the fire of our infantry made it an impossibility to penetrate our lines, although many of the enemy were found dead on our entrenchments. Case shot, shrapnel, and at intervals star shell, were all fired with great effect by the Mountain Battery, the illumination of the latter projectile enabling our infantry to pour in the most deadly volleys into bodies of the enemy, occasionally at a few yards' distance; for so dark was the night, that at any distance over twenty yards' it was impossible to see anything. The enemy soon completely surrounded our camp, and from the hills and ravines around us poured in a steady fire, under cover of which their swordsmen, in spite of all reverses, made repeated rushes, first on one side, then on another, in futile attempts to force an entrance.

We had struck all our tents, and, except when occasion demanded, we all lay flat on the ground, while the camp was meanwhile swept by bullets, a number of them from Martini - Henry and Lee - Metford rifles, which, with a varied assortment of Sniders, Tower muskets, Winchester repeaters, and sporting rifles, and the not-to-be-despised jezail, made up their arsenal, while they evidently possessed no lack of ammunition, the attack being kept up till shortly after 2 A.M., up to which time the fire never slackened. Occasionally a mad fanatical rush would be made, only to be met by a storm of bullets, through which even the Ghazis failed to penetrate. It was rumoured that the tribesmen were so certain of capturing our camp, that they had brought baggage animals to carry away the loot.

Considering the heavy fire we were thus subjected to for five hours, our casualties were light, largely owing to the efficacy of the earthwork we had made round our camp, and to the reserves and all men not employed in manning the defensive work being made to lie down.

Our Brigadier, General Wodehouse, was unfortunately shot at an early phase of the attack, having walked up to confer with Sir Bindon Blood. He was shot through the leg with a Martini-Henry bullet, which, fortunately, missed the bone. Our total casualties during this attack were thirty-two, one other British officer, Veterinary-Captain Mann, and one native officer being wounded, and one British soldier killed. Of the remainder who were wounded, three belonged to the British, and nineteen to the native ranks. Besides these losses, one hundred and fifteen horses and transport animals were killed and wounded.

The enemy's losses were very heavy, numbers of them being found lying dead on our entrenchments the following morning. It was ascertained afterwards that the villages within our vicinity lost three hundred and thirty killed alone, and numbers of dead and wounded must have been carried over the passes to their distant homes; while the contingent from Afghan territory were reported not only to have suffered heavily, but to have lost heart and retired over the border.

The effect of the repulse of the attack,

in the face of the promises made by the two Mullahs to these credulous hillmen, was the rapid dismemberment of the entire gathering, which was reported to have practically dispersed by the 22nd, with the exception of the Hadda Mullah's personal following.

It was a queer scene that presented itself to our eyes when the enemy, shortly after 2 A.M., gave up all hope of rushing our camp, and left us free to count up the cost of the night's events. All the tents were down, looking like so many corpses in the dim light of a rising moon, for even in the hospital it had been found impossible to keep the tents pitched or a light burning, owing to the heavy fire that was at once directed on them, and our wounded lay in rows on the ground, their wounds having been dressed under the combined disadvantages of a pitch dark night and a hailstorm of bullets. On all sides horses and transport animals lay dead and dying, the casualties among animals having been most severe,

THE HADDA MULLAH

especially among the 11th Bengal Lancers,* one of the best mounted native cavalry regiments in India, and the fatality with which one's most cherished pony or charger fell a victim to war on this occasion, leaving the cheap and unvalued hack untouched, proved a subject for lamentation for more than one officer on the following morning.

The last farewell shot having been fired in the distance by the rapidly disappearing foe, the camp soon resumed its normal aspect; and, wrapt in slumber, a peaceful silence, unbroken by aught save the occasional challenge of a sentry, succeeded the discordant noise of the recent combat.

* Late "Probyn's Horse."

CHAPTER XII

ARRIVAL OF GENERAL ELLES — CAPTURE OF THE BEDMANAI PASS — THROUGH THE JAROBI GORGE — THE HADDA MULLAH'S HOME BURNT — FURTHER OPERATIONS IN THE MAMUND VALLEY

THE following day, Sir Bindon Blood met General Elles at Lakerai, and arranged to leave with him our Third Brigade, the command of which had now devolved on Lieutenant-Colonel Graves, 39th Garhwalis, in place of General Wodehouse, who was wounded; and while General Elles thus reinforced could deal with the Hadda Mullah's gathering, General Blood would proceed at once to Inayat Kila to join his Second Brigade, at present engaged under General Jeffreys in the Mamund Valley.

General Elles accordingly took up a

position, with the two brigades he now had at his disposal, at the foot of the Bedmanai Pass, near the village of Kuz Chinarai; and every preparation was made on the night of the 23rd for the attack on the pass the following morning. The troops were in the best of spirits at the prospect of at last getting some reward, in the shape of a good fight, for the arduous marching and road-making they had already undergone. There seemed, too, every chance of the fight proving a stubborn one, for scarcely had "lights out" sounded when the enemy commenced "sniping" heavily into camp. No actual attack on the camp, however, was made, though small parties of tribesmen advanced with great rashness close to the entrenchments. The enemy's efforts, although continued until past midnight, were fruitless, there being no casualties on our side during the night.

The next morning at 6.30 the troops paraded for the attack. The first objective was a low, conical hill and a village at the mouth of the pass, which was found on approach to be occupied by the enemy. General Westmacott's brigade was then entrusted with the further attack on the pass, and General Graves' brigade was told off to guard against a flank attack from the direction of Mittai, where it was known considerable bodies of the enemy were collected. The 20th Punjab Infantry, with the 1st Gurkhas in support, were ordered to make the assault, and to secure the hills commanding the pass.

This was gallantly carried out, the enemy contesting every inch of the ground, but with their numbers evidently much reduced since their defeat and heavy losses at Nawagai, only a small gathering of some eight hundred of them opposed our troops, who, clearing ridge after ridge, finally crowned a peak 2500 feet above the pass. It appeared that the tribal leaders had expected an attack from the direction of the Mittai Valley, and had, consequently, divided their forces. It was shortly after

SHINDANA PASS

CAPTURE OF BEDMANAI PASS 165

midday when the pass and the hills overlooking it were in our hands, and this assault had been accomplished with a loss of only two men killed and three wounded all belonging to the 20th Punjab Infantry. The Hadda Mullah fled from the field at a very early phase of the action; but the Suffi Mullah was seen constantly rallying his fugitive followers, with, however, but small success. After the capture of the pass, General Westmacott's brigade advanced to Bedmanai village, and encamped there; whilst General Graves brigade returned to camp near Kuz Chinarai.

On the 25th, the former brigade marched to Tor Khel, a village situated at the mouth of the Jarobi gorge, through which this force was shortly to penetrate and wreak a well-merited vengeance on the home of the Hadda Mullah. This gorge was a veritable death-trap; with precipitous cliffs on either side, the crests of which were well wooded with pine and walnut-trees, it would have been an awkward place to force if held by a few determined foes. Luckily, the opposition was slight, and a small force under General Elles pushed through, burning the towers and forts of what formerly constituted the Hadda Mullah's sanctuary. The retirement to camp, however, proved a far harder task, the tribesmen harassing the force returning through the narrow gorge, and had not the troops been handled with great skill, the losses would have indeed been heavy. Our total casualties during the day's operations were one man killed and seventeen wounded. During the following night, there was the usual desultory firing into camp, which resulted in two sepoys being wounded and a camel-driver killed.

On the 26th the force marched to Lakerai, and thence *via* the Gandab valley, towards Peshawar, where they were merged into the Tirah Field Force, which was about to start operations against the Afridis.

In the meantime, Sir Bindon Blood, with the headquarter staff and two squadrons 11th Bengal Lancers, had arrived at Inayat

Kila, where he found General Jeffreys' brigade still engaged in operations against the Mamunds, who, in spite of the punishment they had received, were still obdurate. The land occupied by this clan lies partly over the border within Afghan territory, and to this fact may be assigned one reason, and perhaps the chief one, for the long-continued obstinacy with which they held out against our troops; refusing point-blank to comply with our terms, which included the restoration of the sixteen rifles taken during the recent action on the 16th. They admitted having taken part in the attack on Chakdara, and in defence of their action on that occasion they naïvely gave the old and oft-repeated excuse of having only followed the example of the rest of the world.

With the inconceivable conceit of the Pathan, they offered in reparation for their misdeeds a few useless old jezails and firearms, which might have been of some value to a collecter of antique relics, but from a military point of view would have been gladly left in the hands of our enemies if they could have been persuaded to use them. The Mamunds had indeed proved their courage in many a hard-fought action, but it is doubtful if they could have produced a warrior bold enough to fire off any one of the various firearms they were good enough to surrender on this occasion.

Hostilities were accordingly continued. On the 22nd, part of the force marched up the valley to a village named Dag, whence we brought back fodder and grain; our retirement being followed up by the enemy, who made no attempt, however, to come to close quarters. We had one man in the Guides killed, and two in the 35th Sikhs wounded.

The next day we attacked the fortified village of Tangi, taking with us a considerable number of transport animals. The enemy appeared at first in small numbers, but by this time we had learnt with what remarkable rapidity their numbers increased as they swarmed round to harass our retirement. The position was soon cap-

CAPTURE OF BEDMANAI PASS

tured, and the transport mules having been loaded with immense quantities of grain and fodder, found as usual buried and hidden away in the village, the retirement was commenced under cover of the guns, which effectually prevented the tribesmen closing in. Major Moody, of the Buffs, received a wound in the neck, which, slight as it was at the time, caused him considerable inconvenience afterwards. Lieutenant Reeves of the same regiment had a rather curious escape, a bullet striking his revolver and glancing off through his belts.

The Buffs, who had been ordered to join the Tirah Field Force, left us on the 25th, much to the regret of our force, a regret which the Mamunds could not have shared; for the regiment, under the trying conditions of this guerilla warfare, had fully maintained its reputation, earned by some two centuries of distinguished service.

A cessation of hostilities now occurred for a few days, as the tribesmen had sent in to ask our terms. The jirga, which was interviewed by our political officers, Mr Davies and Mr Gunter, brought in Rs. 4000; but on hearing that our terms insisted on the restoration of the captured rifles, stated that these had gone over the border and were unobtainable. They were given up to the 29th to accede to our terms; and in the meantime Sir Bindon Blood, having been ordered to proceed at once to Peshawar to assume command of the 1st Division Tirah Field Force, marched to Panjkora, which he had no sooner reached than news of such a disquieting nature arrived from the Mamund valley that he was forthwith obliged to return there. The outlook in this region was by no means a peaceful one.

In spite of their sending in a jirga to negotiate, it appeared that the Mamunds had no intention of submitting; and, having obtained a large supply of rifle ammunition and some reinforcements from their friends over the border, they were now prepared for a fresh campaign.

CHAPTER XIII

ATTACK ON AGRAH AND GAT—ARRIVAL OF FIELD BATTERY AND HIGHLAND LIGHT INFANTRY — SKIRMISH AT BADELAI — RAHIM SHAH

THE geographical position of this petty tribe undoubtedly lent itself to a long and protracted warfare; being situated on the border, the tribesmen who occupied land within Afghan territory, were in a most secure and happy position. With that neighbourly solicitude which is one of the chief characteristics of these Asiatic people, they were able to cross the border and bring their forces to the assistance of the Mamunds, whom they thus lured on into hostilities with our troops, with the comforting assurance that if repulsed, they could retire back to their homes, secure from the retribution which would certainly overtake their friends on this side of the border; while success, on the other hand, opened glorious visions of a massacre of the infidel, with a share in the rich loot to be afterwards obtained.

General Jeffreys had now recommenced operations. On the 30th September an attack in force was made on the fortified villages of Agrah and Gat. These two villages occupied the strongest strategical position of any we had yet seen; perched on the lower slope of a steep and rugged hill, and mutually supporting each other, they were protected on either side by high rocky spurs, while the rough boulders and loose stones which strewed the foreground foretold an arduous climb for our attacking infantry. As we marched up the valley, the tom-toms of the tribesmen could be heard with great distinctness in the still morning air; and as we approached nearer, we could gradually make out their forces holding the spurs and high cliffs commanding the villages.

To our left lay an offshoot to the valley, covered with scrub jungle, down which large numbers of the enemy could be seen hastening to join their comrades. This was soon checked, however, by the appearance of our cavalry, two squadrons of the Guides under Colonel Adams, effectually keeping at bay over a thousand Ghazis. Unaccustomed to horses, these tribesmen have the most exaggerated notions of the power of cavalry; and on this occasion, in spite of the high jungle and the ground being utterly unsuitable for cavalry movements, they would not venture anywhere within striking distance.

The village of Agrah was the first to be attacked. A glance at the enemy's position had made it obvious that the spurs on either side must be captured before the village commanded by them could be successfully stormed. The Guides Infantry were therefore ordered to clear the spur to the left; the 31st Punjab Infantry, supported by the 38th Dogras, the centre ridge between the two villages, while the Royal West Kent advanced straight up the hill on the right of the Guides.

On the advance taking place, the Pathan and Afridi companies of the Guides dashed up the hill with a wild yell, which intimidated the tribesmen to such an extent, that although they poured in a heavy fire, this spur was taken without a single casualty, while many of the enemy were shot down in their panic-stricken flight from the crest.

The ridge up which the 31st were stubbornly fighting their way was by no means so easily taken. The ground consisted, for the most part, of high-terraced fields, commanded by strongly-built sungars amongst the huge boulders at the top, and it was here that Colonel O'Brien fell mortally wounded while gallantly leading on his men to the assault. In spite of their commanding officer being killed, the 31st pushed on under the covering fire of Major Fegan's Mountain Battery; these guns, with the greatest precision, dropping

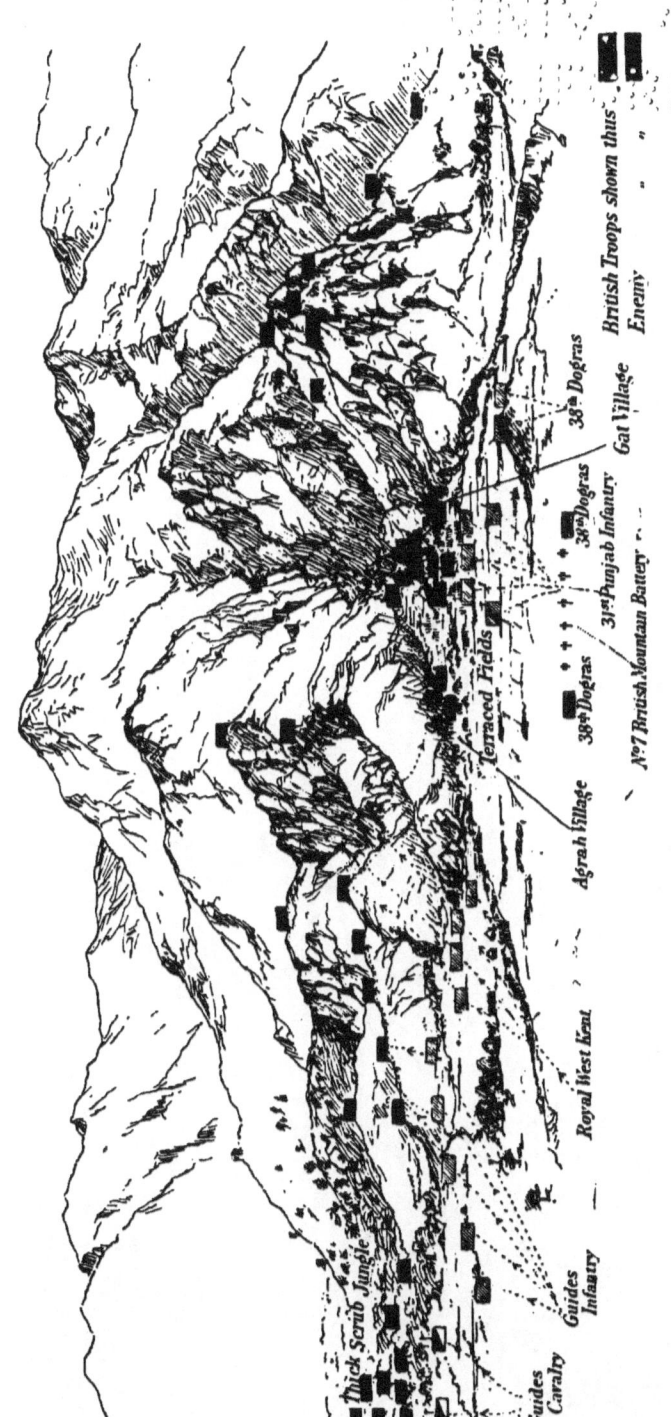

SKETCH OF ATTACK ON AGRAH AND GAT

CALIPER

ATTACK ON AGRAH AND GAT

shell after shell amongst the Mamunds, who, although having lost heavily, still stuck manfully to their position, and as many of the huge rocks and boulders proved impervious to artillery fire, it was only the bayonets of our sepoys that finally turned them out.

The 31st were now joined by the West Kent, who came down from the spur on the left, burning the village of Agrah on their way, and proceeded to drive the enemy out of several strong positions above the village of Gat. It was here that half a company of the West Kent, on reaching a sungar, were suddenly charged by a lot of Ghazis, and in the melée which ensued, many of the West Kents were killed and wounded, their officer, 2nd Lieutenant Browne Clayton, being one of the first to be cut down, his body being almost at once recovered by a gallant dash under Major Western.

Owing to the day being far spent, it was impossible to attempt any further operations. The troops had not only a march of some ten miles to make before reaching camp, but there was also before them that most difficult of all tasks, the retirement down hill in the presence of a brave and fanatical foe. Hampered with their wounded, and assailed on all sides by a storm of bullets, the slightest appearance of confusion or hurry on the part of our rear-guard would cause the enemy to swoop down in overwhelming force. On this occasion the steady fire of our men, as they worked their way with a slow deliberation down hill, enabled us to reach the welcome plain below with but few casualties, and the Mamunds, contrary to their usual tactics, forbore to follow up our retirement to camp that evening.

Our casualties this day were 61 : among these the somewhat disproportionate number of eight British officers being killed and wounded. The service had lost two officers who could ill be spared in Colonel O'Brien and Lieutenant Browne Clayton, both of

ATTACK ON AGRAH AND GAT

whom died, however, in the manner best fitted to a soldier—at the head of the men they were so gallantly leading.

Six officers had been wounded—namely, Major Western, Captains R. C. Style and N. H. Lowe, Lieutenants H. Isacke (severely) and F. A. Jackson of the Royal West Kent, and Lieutenant E. B. Peacock, 31st Punjab Infantry.

Two days' rest were now given to the force, a rest which was very welcome after the fighting of the last fortnight. Sir Bindon Blood, who had now transferred his headquarters to Inayat Kila, had ordered up the Field Battery and Highland Light Infantry, the latter regiment having the bad luck to arrive on the evening of the 3rd October, the day which was destined to witness the last of our attacks on the Mamund villages.

Our objective this day was "Badelai," a village which, owing to its position, lent itself to a strategic movement on our part, which proved a complete success. General

Jeffreys led the force straight up the valley in the direction of Agrah, the village where the severe fighting of three days back had occurred, and towards which the enemy commenced streaming from all parts of the valley. Not until we had passed Badelai, which lay to our right, was the direction of the head of the column changed. The tribesmen were thus completely thrown off the scent, and our sudden march on Badelai must have come as a surprise to them. Our attack was almost unopposed, and the village had been burnt before the enemy's forces arrived on the scene: even then they were unable to work round the hills in time to harass our retirement until the level plain had been reached. In revenge, they attempted to follow us up during our return to camp, but soon discovered that the level ground gave us many advantages over them, advantages which had been hitherto balanced by their superior mobility on the hill-side. Their losses on this day must have been heavy, owing to the boldness with which they advanced over the open ground, affording a good target to our two Mountain Batteries. Our casualties were very light,—two men being killed and sixteen wounded.

Fighting is the principal recreation and amusement of these hardy tribesmen, but recent events had evidently shown them that certain pleasures can be too dearly bought, and unless peace was soon restored, there would soon be nothing left to them of their homes and villages. A truce was accordingly declared, while negotiations were carried on through the Khans of Nawagai, Khar and Jhar, the three principal chiefs in Bajour, while one of the men in the employ of the political department was sent up the valley to interview the Mamund Maliks.

This man, "Rahim Shah," had done good service during the Chitral campaign, and had in many ways proved invaluable to our political officers. He belonged to the

Kaka Khel tribe or rather family, there being only about a couple of hundred of these people in existence. Their history is a curious one: being descendants of a famous saint, they have a free pass over the whole country; no small boon among such a lawless people, and which they had made good use of for trading purposes.

The sanctity of their persons is well shown by the following incident, which occurred during our stay. In spite of the truce, one of our foraging parties had come into collision with the tribesmen, who had laid an ambush for our men, which fortunately only resulted in one man being wounded. During the skirmish which ensued, Rahim Shah, alone and unarmed, at the mercy of the most fanatical race in the world, was arranging terms with the remainder of the tribe; and, although known to be in our employ, was treated with the greatest respect, arriving a few days later with the jirga, who came offering general submission.

CHAPTER XIV

CESSATION OF HOSTILITIES — A DURBAR — DEPARTURE TO THE SALARZAI VALLEY — RECONNAISSANCE TO PASHAT — SUBMISSION OF TRIBES

A FEW days later came the end. The Maliks and the majority of the tribesmen were ready to submit, and although the younger and more hot-blooded portion of the community wished to continue a war which must eventually have resulted in the extermination of the clan, negotiations were finally brought to a successful issue through the influence of the Khan of Nawagai and his brother.

A durbar was held on the 11th, at a spot not far distant from our camp. Here, under a clump of shady Chenar trees, Sir Bindon Blood, accompanied by Major

Deane and the Khans of Nawagai, Jhar and Khar, interviewed the Maliks and head men of the Mamund district. Major Deane began by asking them if they wanted peace or war; with the exception of one or two Maliks, whose villages had already been punished, and who, having also had their grain taken by our troops, thought they had nothing further to lose, the Mamunds were unanimously in favour of peace, and they expressed regret for the fighting which had already occurred. They further stated that they had suffered heavy losses, and were now willing to surrender the rifles they had captured. Besides this, they promised that Umra Khan's following, and all the men who had joined them from over the Afghan border, should be turned out of their valley. It was considered that the damage done to their villages during the month's hostilities was sufficient punishment, and amply settled all outstanding accounts with the clan; so, security having been taken for the rifles,

CESSATION OF HOSTILITIES 183

peace was concluded, and the jirga dismissed.

In the course of the almost continuous fighting which had taken place during our stay in this valley, we had captured, together with all their hoarded stores of grain, twenty-six villages, of which we had destroyed the fortifications and towers. This latter punishment is felt by these people even more acutely than the loss of their grain; for the wood, which is an essential feature in the construction of these buildings, is extremely scarce and difficult to obtain, trees in these desolate and bleak highlands being few and far between. The losses we inflicted on them are difficult to estimate, for a large number of the men opposed to us in the field had come from neighbouring tribes and from Afghan territory, but they must have been very severe.

Success, however, had been purchased at some cost to ourselves, for our casualties during the recent fighting had been exceptionally heavy, owing to the difficulties of the ground and inaccessibility of the villages, built among the crags and peaks of the steep hills; in the guerilla warfare, incident on operations over ground of this description, the individual prowess of these hardy tribesmen, trained to the use of their arms from childhood, and imbued with an hereditary instinct for fighting derived from generations of warlike ancestors, almost counterbalanced the superior combination and handling of our more highly-disciplined troops, and we soon learnt that our opponents were by no means to be despised. Armed with every variety of firearm, including Martini-Henry rifles made in Cabul, or in some cases stolen from our troops, Sniders, sporting-rifles, and old Tower muskets, these hillmen would swarm down on our troops during our retirement to camp, and, taking advantage of cover from every rock and stone *en route*, would pour in a deadly fire at close quarters. In fighting of this sort, firing by volleys proved useless and a mere waste of valuable ammunition, while our crack shots, accustomed to taking

SNIPING THE CAMP AT NIGHT

a deliberate aim at a more or less clearly defined object, were at a disadvantage when compelled to rely solely on snap-shots taken at a rapidly moving foe.

On the 13th of October the Mamund Valley was evacuated, our force moving to Matashah, whence we proceeded to deal with the Salarzais, a section of the Bajour tribe. Two days were given to these people to bring in the number of firearms demanded of them, as a punishment for the share they had taken in the Swat rising; and in the meantime, while hostilities were suspended, reconnaissances were pushed up the valley, which appeared far more fertile and open than we had expected from our late experiences, while an abundant supply of water would enable us to camp right up in the heart of their country, close to the scene of operations, should war be necessary. Many of their villages were in the lower parts of the valley, easily accessible to our troops, and it was evident that little opposition could be offered to a force provided with artillery. During one of our trips up the valley, we were surprised to find ourselves accosted by a dirty-looking ruffian, who greeted us with a "Good morning, sir," in very fair English, and who, on inquiry, proved to have been employed for ten years as a coolie on a sugar plantation in Demarara.

In spite of our being presumably at peace with these people, our camp was fired into every night. This was probably due to the Maliks being unable to keep the "budmashes" and malcontents of the tribe quiet, and we were fortunate in that the bullet rarely found its billet. The chief difficulty was in providing shelter for the animals, and although traverses were usually built at each end of a line of horses or mules, it was impossible to protect them entirely from stray bullets. Altogether these snipers caused us a good deal of annoyance, for not only did they wake up the whole camp, but the friendly piquets belonging to the Khan of Nawagai,

UNIV. OF
CALIFORNI

PUSHAT, SALAZAI VALLEY

CESSATION OF HOSTILITIES 187

who were usually posted round our camp with a view to keeping these gentlemen off, made such a noise among themselves, firing their rifles and shouting directions to each other, that although the original cause of all this disturbance may not have done much damage, he had certainly succeeded by that time in destroying our night's rest.

On the 15th, a reconnaissance in force was made to within two miles of Pashat, a large village, of which the principal feature was a strong fort. This village was evidently the metropolis of the neighbourhood, and was situated in the most fertile portion of the valley, surrounded on all sides by fields of young crops of barley and wheat, which were watered by a considerable river. The inhabitants were peaceably following their agricultural pursuits, and with their women and children about, and their herds of cattle grazing at the foot of the hills, it was evident they did not mean to fight. This was shortly afterwards proved by the appearance of a jirga, who brought with them the required arms.

Some delay had been caused owing to disputes between the Upper and Lower Salarzais; the villages in the hills and the upper portion of the valley having objected to handing over their share of the imposed penalty; but pressure having been brought to bear on them by the remainder of the clan, no recourse to arms on our part proved necessary.

CHAPTER XV

COMMISSARIAT AND TRANSPORT ARRANGEMENTS—EXPEDITION INTO UTMAN KHEL COUNTRY—RETURN TO THE MALAKAND

BEFORE leaving the neighbourhood of Matashah, the Shamozai section of the Utman Khel tribe remained to be dealt with. This clan inhabits the valleys and hill-sides to the south of the Bajour stream below Khar, and had maintained an insolent attitude towards the Government, refusing so far to make any terms of submission. During the Chitral Expedition, they had been suspected of joining the Bajouris and other tribes of this part in attacks on our lines of communication, and there was no doubt as to their complicity in the recent attack on Chakdara. During the advance of the force to Nawagai, the political officer had been in communication with their Maliks, but nothing had come of it; and as it was of the greatest importance that the column should reach the Mohmand country as quickly as possible, there was then no opportunity of enforcing our terms on the tribe. As the force marched up the valley, their villages and towers offered a most tempting target for our guns, and no one would have been sorry if an excuse to "go for" them had been given; but they kept perfectly neutral, and did not even attack our convoys, though they were credited with such sniping as occurred round the camp at Jhar on our return march.

In order to be nearer the Shamozai villages, we moved to our old encampment at Jhar, from whence negotiations could be carried out with greater facility; but, before leaving the Salarzai valley, it was decided to punish a certain Malik who not only had kept up a position of continued hostility towards us, but had also encouraged the malcontents to fire nightly into our camp, whereby, on the last night at Matasah, a sowar of the Guides Cavalry had been wounded. Some towers and fortified buildings belonging to this Malik were, therefore, destroyed by the Sappers, and the reports of these buildings being blown up announced our final evacuation of the Salarzai Valley.

Early next day the Shamozai "jirga" arrived, and was met outside the camp by the political officers. Their consultation resulted in the tribe agreeing to all our terms, and the guns and rifles demanded of them were brought in the same day.

The total collapse of the Salarzai and Shamozai clans was rather unexpected, but it followed quite naturally on the submission of the Mamunds, who are looked up to by their neighbours as being the most formidable of all the tribes along this portion of the frontier. It was from the ranks of these bold warriors that the notorious chieftain, "Umra Khan," drew the pick of his fighting men.

On the news of the Shamozai submission, orders were issued for the march of the force next day towards Panjkora. We were not to depart without a final salute from the "snipers," who fired several shots into camp at night, but without doing any damage, being eventually driven off by the friendly Jhar piquets.

We marched into Chakdara on the 24th October, leaving the First Brigade at Panjkora to wait until the large quantities of commissariat stores which had been collected there should be removed to our depot at Khar. In spite of the hard work our transport animals had undergone, there were remarkably few that were unfit for duty.

On all frontier expeditions, the Indian Commissariat Transport Department has many difficulties to contend with. To fully appreciate these, it must be remembered that seldom if ever can wheeled transport be employed, owing to the entire absence of roads, and that all the supplies consumed by a force in the field have to be carried with it, or to it, on pack animals. Nothing but grain, fuel, and fodder can ever be procured on the spot, and these frequently are not obtainable in any quantities. The country operated in offers many difficulties; the steep and rocky hill tracks often requiring much improvement with pick and shovel before they are rendered feasible for the passage of mules and camels.

In the official scheme for the Malakand Field Force, the transport allotted was what is known as the "Normal Scale." This means a certain number of mules, called "obligatory" mules, for the carriage of what it is important should remain close to a regiment under all circumstances, such as water, pack-alls, entrenching tools, first reserve ammunition, etc.; and camels for the rest of the regimental impedimenta. In addition, camel transport was provided for the carriage of five days' rations for men and two days' grain for animals; and it was apparently never contemplated when the scheme was drawn up that the troops would have to remain for more than five days at a time away from the advanced depot.

For the line of communication a cart train of Government bullock-carts was arranged from Nowshera to Malakand four stages; and also a dak of 60 tongas was laid out for running back the sick and wounded from the Field Hospitals to the base. The total transport thus provided was:—

Mules, 3547.
Camels, 3864.
Carts, 640. (These were used eventually as far as Chakdara.)
Tongas, 143. (These came as far as Panjkora.)

As brigades had frequently to operate in a country unsuited to camel transport, it was found necessary to redistribute the transport allotted. One brigade would be equipped entirely with mule carriage, handing over its camels to one of the other

RETURN TO THE MALAKAND 195

brigades, which would thus be equipped almost entirely with camel transport. This arrangement continued almost throughout the expedition; the transport being exchanged between brigades when required.

In all frontier expeditions sufficient time is usually given to admit of all supplies and transport being collected at the station fixed upon as the base of operations; and all units start from there fully equipped, field-service clothing being generally issued to corps and units before they leave their stations for the front. In this instance, however, the urgent necessity of pushing troops up to relieve the garrisons of Malakand and Chakdara, which were hardly pressed by the enemy, did not admit of matters being dealt with in this manner, and the commissariat* department were thus hard put to it at first to find carriage and supplies for the troops as they arrived. Supplies for thirty days for the whole force

* The Chief Commissariat Officer with the force was Major Wharry, D.S.O. Captain Thackwell was Divisional Transport Officer.

had been collected at Khar, in the Swat Valley, by the 15th August.

When it was decided that two brigades from this force were to march *via* the Bajour Valley through Mohmund territory, to co-operate with the Mohmund Field Force, and to debouch at Shabkadr, fresh commissariat - transport arrangements became necessary. Supply depots had to be formed at Chakdara and Panjkora, and troops were located at the different stages up to the latter place to protect convoys. No further transport was, however, allotted for the extended line of communication; and the extra work had to be performed with what had been provided for operations in the Swat Valley. The line of communication being thus considerably lengthened, supplies had to be stored at Panjkora, so that the two brigades might start from there fully equipped, one carrying ten days' rations for men and two days' grain for animals, and the second carrying fifteen days' rations for men and the same as the other brigade for animals. These supplies were intended to carry the brigades through to Shabkadr; and as the force advanced, it was cut off from its line of communication, which were then withdrawn towards Malakand.

Subsequent events, however, upset all these arrangements. One brigade was halted at Nawagai, three marches from Panjkora, awaiting the arrival of the Mohmund Field Force; and the other had to undertake active operations against the Mamunds. This necessitated the re-opening of the Panjkora depot, from which place the commissariat supplied both these brigades for two months.

On the return of the troops to the Swat Valley, the mules were in excellent condition. The camel transport* had suffered somewhat, as on them had fallen the brunt

---

* In the 1895 campaign the Chitral Relief Force consisted of about 16,000 men, for which transport was provided of a lifting power of 124,250 maunds (1 maund = 80 lbs.). In the present campaign, for a force of 12,000 men, a lifting power of 32,315 maunds only was allotted.

of the work of keeping the Panjkora depot replenished and conveying supplies to the front. Moreover, camels as a rule are never worked by their owners during the months of August and September, which are looked on as the "off season" for these animals, when they are turned out to graze.

The total casualties during the period of operations were as follows :—

Mules, 66, of which 35 were killed in action.
Camels, 368, of which 6 were killed in action.

Whilst the number of animals temporarily unfit for work at the close of the operations was—

Mules, 52, of which 29 were from bullet wounds.
Camels, 98.

Operations were now over: at least for some time to come.

Owing to the progress of events in Tirah, our force was kept mobilised near the Malakand for over two months, inactive with the exception of a small force * which

* Buffs, 21st Punjab Infantry, 35th Sikhs, No. 8 Bengal Mountain Battery, one squadron 10th Bengal Lancers, No. 5 Company Madras Sappers and Miners.

RETURN TO THE MALAKAND 199

was despatched under Colonel Reid to deal with those sections of the Utman Khel tribe on the left bank of the Swat River who had not yet complied with our terms. These consisted of a fine of two thousand rupees, and the surrendering of all rifles, three hundred guns and three hundred swords.

Colonel Reid's force concentrated at Utman Khel Garhi on the 22nd November, crossed the Barh Pass on the 24th, and marched to Kot, where all the representative jirgas tendered their submission and accepted our terms, with the exception of the people of Agrah, to which place a flying column, consisting of a thousand men and two guns, were despatched on the 28th. On arrival there, our terms were at once complied with, and so the force returned once more to the Malakand.

Thus ended our four months' wanderings in a land full of interest, both as regards people and country. The former, although barbarous and uncivilised, had shown a courage and knowledge of warfare that it is to be hoped will at some not far distant period be turned to good account: and these hardy mountaineers, instead of being, as at present, a perpetual source of anxiety on our frontier, may prove one of the greatest safeguards of our Indian Empire.

CHAPTER XVI

INVASION OF BUNER—ATTACK ON THE TANGI AND PIRSAI PASSES—PIR BABA ZARIAT—CLOSE OF THE CAMPAIGN

IN spite of the peaceable aspect of this portion of the Indian frontier since the termination of the events afore recorded, the Fates had decreed that we should not yet disperse to our various homes. For the tribes of Buner and Chamla, inhabiting the mountainous country to the south-east of Swat, refused to comply with the punitive terms imposed on them by the Indian Government for their complicity in the recent attack on the Malakand. Both these tribes had also sent large contingents to oppose our advance into the upper Swat Valley, and were reported to have lost heavily at Landakai.

The terms imposed on these two tribes were as follow :—

On Buner.

1. Submission of a representative jirga of all sections to be made.
2. Restoration of all Government property.
3. Surrender of 600 firearms, including all breech-loaders and Enfield rifles stolen from the Rustam border.
4. Payment of cash fine of Rs. 11.500.

The Chamla people were ordered to surrender 100 firearms, and pay a fine of Rs. 1500.

The seven days which had been granted to the tribesmen within which to accede to these terms having elapsed, Government despatched a force under Major-General Sir Bindon Blood, K.C.B., to invade Buner.

This force, which was officially termed the Buner Field Force, consisted of two brigades, with some divisional troops.

First Brigade (commanded by Brigadier-General Meiklejohn, C.M.G., C.B.)—

1st Battalion, Royal West Kent Regiment.

16th Regiment of Bengal Infantry.
20th (Punjab) Regiment of Bengal Infantry.
31st (Punjab) Regiment of Bengal Infantry.

Second Brigade (commanded by Brigadier-General Jeffreys, C.B.)—

1st Battalion, East Kent Kegiment.
The Corps of Guides Infantry.
21st (Punjab) Regiment of Bengal Infantry.

Divisional Troops.

The 10th Field Battery, Royal Artillery.
No. 7 Mountain Battery, Royal Artillery.
No. 8 (Bengal) Mountain Battery.
4 Squadrons of Cavalry, to be detailed from the Corps of Guides Cavalry and the 10th Bengal Lancers.
3rd Bombay Infantry.
No. 4 Company, Bengal Sappers and Miners.
No. 5 Company, Madras Sappers and Miners.
2nd Battalion, Highland Light Infantry.

The passes leading into Buner having been well reconnoitred, General Blood's dispositions for attack were as follow:—

The main attack was to be delivered at the Tangi Pass. All the approaches into the country lay over high and precipitous passes, and the Tangi was selected as not only being tactically the easiest to capture, but also, looking to the subsequent plan of campaign in this country, it occupied by far the best strategical position, lending itself, moreover, to a manœuvre which proved most successful.

It was intended that at the same time as the assault on the Tangi was delivered, a small column, consisting of two battalions infantry and five squadrons cavalry, should endeavour, by surprising the enemy, to effect an entrance into the country over the Pirsai Pass. Both these passes opened on their farther side into narrow valleys leading directly into each other. The defenders of either pass were thus liable to have their line of retreat cut off, and to be attacked in rear by whichever force penetrated into their country.

To carry out this scheme, a column under the command of Colonel Adams, V.C., composed of the Guides Infantry, 31st Punjab Infantry, three squadrons 10th Bengal Lancers and two squadrons Guides Cavalry, was sent to Rustam.

This place threatened three different passes leading into Buner—namely, the Ambéla, the Malandri, and the Pirsai; the latter being our objective.

Thus, from Rustam, Colonel Adams' force could attack any one of these passes, which were within a few miles of each other, but on the farther side, from the geographical formation of the hill ranges, these passes were practically two days' march. The tribesmen, not knowing which one our force would attempt, were obliged to hold all three, and on the day of attack were unable to assemble in any force: more than two-thirds of their strength being isolated on the Malandri and Ambéla.

The greater portion of the fighting men had assembled on the Tangi, at the foot of which Sir Bindon Blood encamped his two brigades on Thursday, the 6th January, prior to the attack which was to take place the following morning.

From the village of Sanghao, near which the camp was situated, a fairly good road ran the whole way into Mardan, greatly facilitating the transport thus far.

The actual assault of the pass was given to General Meiklejohn, who took the position with only one casualty.

The 20th Punjab Infantry were the first in the field, being directed to make a turning movement, ascending a spur about a mile to the left, and finally crowning a peak some 500 feet higher than the pass itself. The Royal West Kent and 16th Bengal Infantry advanced up the path which was ordinarily used by the natives of the country; while the Highland Light Infantry, with the 21st Punjab Infantry on their right, climbed up the spurs leading on to the pass; this frontal attack was covered by artillery fire, besides the well-directed volleys with which the Buffs and 3rd Bombay Infantry, who remained as escort to the guns, swept the face of the hill, making it impossible for the tribesmen to collect in sufficient numbers to rush down on our advancing infantry. The crest of the pass, some 600 yards long, was

UNIV.
CALIF.

THE TANGI PASS. 7TH MOUNTAIN BATTERY IN ACTION

fortunately well commanded by the Field Battery at a range of 2200 yards, while the two Mountain Batteries came into action at a distance between 1600 and 2000 yards from a spur of the hill facing the pass, and about 500 feet above its foot. The effect of these three batteries can well be imagined. Opening fire about 9 A.M., they sent a storm of shrapnel all along the ridge, making it almost impossible for the tribesmen to show themselves over the crest line. Gradually the numerous standards which lined the heights, floating so bravely in the morning air, went down, their bearers either shot or unable to stand longer the hailstorm of bullets. One or two individuals, inspired by the spirit of Ghazism, dashed out from amongst their comrades, to die in their vain but plucky attempt to get to close quarters with our men, who were so occupied indeed with climbing the almost precipitous slopes and cliffs, that it was lucky for them that they were able to do so under such favourable circumstances. The

20th had the stiffest climb, the peak which they finally had to ascend appearing absolutely impregnable, with a piquet of the enemy on the top. These, however, evidently never expected an attack from this quarter, and the effect of this regiment coming down on their flank, driving before them the small parties which attempted to oppose them, was very disconcerting. Led by Colonel Woon, the 20th had got up unperceived, and gained possession of a sungar, which was held by a small piquet of the tribesmen, before the latter were prepared to meet them. The peak carried, the defence of the pass soon collapsed; the tribesmen hurrying down the hill to escape the fire which harassed their retreat. The only casualty during the advance of our men up the hillside was one man of the Highland Light Infantry, who, mortally wounded, died the following day.

The troops making the frontal attack would not have got up thus easily had it not been for the turning of the enemy's right flank; for the latter part of the ascent, being commanded by a high rocky peak on the right of the pass, the tribesmen were able to roll down rocks and stones on our men, which would have certainly added considerably to their difficulties had the former been able to retain this position.

The summit being reached, the troops gave three cheers, which were echoed back by the snow-clad peaks and mountains of Buner, as a welcome to these the first British troops ever to enter the country. General Meiklejohn now pushed on with his brigade to Kingargali, a large village in the valley below, some two miles distant, where he spent the night; the deserted houses affording comfortable quarters for the troops, who found plenty to eat among the goats and chickens with which the village was stocked.

Meanwhile Colonel Adams, having well reconnoitred the three passes from Rustam the previous day, had successfully attacked and taken the Pirsai Pass. The tribesmen, having imagined that his attack would be made by either the Malandri or Ambéla, had sent a strong force to hold both these passes, in consequence of which our task at the Pirsai was far easier than we anticipated. The infantry bivouacked the evening before at the foot of the pass; the cavalry remaining at Rustam to mislead the enemy as to our real point of attack. Unlike the Tangi, this pass was covered by dense jungle up to its crest, and would have proved an extremely difficult task if held by a determined enemy. A couple of standards flaunted their defiance of us, but these were soon lowered, and the infantry arrived at the top about noon, the advance having commenced at 8 A.M. As soon as they gained the crest, the cavalry began to advance up the very narrow and rocky mountain track which constituted the only road over the pass. The ascent was difficult, but the descent on the farther side proved far more so, as, sheltered from the sun, the whole face of the hill was hard frozen, and the path soon became as slippery as ice. The pass itself was 3700 feet above the level of the sea, and the heights on either side were covered with snow. It took some time to get the five squadrons over, every man having to lead his horse walking in single file. On our arrival at the foot, we found we had a narrow and stony defile over three miles in length before the open valley beyond was reached. This was the dry bed of a river, and was covered with huge boulders and rocks; consequently our progress was slow as we advanced along it, a portion of the infantry clearing the way. By the time we arrived at Koui, a small village at the mouth of the defile, it was beginning to get dark: we therefore retraced our steps, and bivouacked for the night at the foot of the pass with the infantry. No baggage had been able to come over, and having nothing but what we carried on our saddles, we passed a very cold and uncomfortable night. But the enemy left us undisturbed. It is probable that they, hardy mountaineers as they are, and accustomed to their severe winters, were hardly prepared to spend the night out on the hillside during a hard frost for the pleasure of sniping or attacking us. Anyhow, not a shot was fired as we sat round a fire, too cold to attempt to sleep, waiting for the dawn which would enable us to move on.

The welcome light finally appearing, we were soon in our saddles, and leaving the infantry to hold the pass, pushed on into the valley below.

Not a sign of the enemy was to be seen. On arriving at a large village in the main valley, we obtained heliographic communication with General Meiklejohn's brigade, who were still encamped at Kingargali, and to this village, after first reconnoitring the country for some distance, we made our way, taking up our quarters for the night alongside this force.

The Bunerwals had hitherto been

thoroughly satisfied with the inaccessibility of their country, surrounded as it is by high snow-clad mountains, and enjoying a reputation as being impregnable; a reputation enhanced, if anything, by the Ambéla campaign. The people, moreover, regarded themselves as being protected from invasion by their patron saint the Pir Baba, who, up to now, had kept inviolate the sanctity of the country. The sudden appearance of our two forces, who had thus so rudely lifted the curtain and penetrated into the heart of the land, completely disconcerted them, causing the utter collapse of the whole tribe.

The next few days were spent in reconnoitring the country, while the rough track over the Tangi was being made feasible by the Sappers and Miners for our transport and baggage to come over. This was soon accomplished, and in spite of the steep ascent, mules were passed over at the rate of 200 per hour. Camels were unable to cross at all, and the Pirsai Pass proved so difficult that a large number of the baggage animals of the detached column were obliged to go round and cross the Tangi. The country which we had now entered, belonged to the Amazai section of the Bunerwals. This being the most powerful and influential of the clans, and occupying a leading position in tribal politics, they were largely responsible for the share the Bunerwals took in the late rising; but now, with a brigade in their country, they were most subservient, and at once complied with the terms imposed. Jirgas also came in from all the adjacent villages, and by the 13th January the remaining sections had sent in their submission. The Hindustani fanatics made an attempt to raise the country, advancing with a small gathering as far as Amnawar; but the Second Brigade, under General Jeffreys, being despatched from Sanghao to the foot of the Ambéla Pass, effectually dispersed them. At the same time, Sir Bindon Blood, with the First Brigade and some of the Divisional troops, marched through the country, halting at certain places in order to collect the money and arms required from the various sections, finally crossing over the Buner Pass into the Chamla Valley, where he was met by General Jeffreys, who brought his brigade over the Ambéla without opposition. The march through Buner was uneventful, although interesting in many ways. The scenery was grand, being more like Switzerland than the Indian Frontier.

The villages we passed differed in one respect from those of Swat and Bajour, being built among shady clumps of trees devoid of towers or defences of any sort: whereas those of their neighbours were invariably strongly fortified and built with a view to the tactical possibilities or rather probabilities of attack.

It would thus seem that, in spite of their reputation, these people were, in reality, less warlike than their neighbours; and although their country was admirably adapted to the guerilla warfare so ably carried on by the Mamunds, the Bunerwals, having made a stand at the passes to prevent the invasion of their country, had now accepted the inevitable, and were not inclined to continue a long and protracted warfare.

The mad fakir to whose inflammatory harangues the rising in Swat was directly due originally came from a small village in the Barandu Valley, through which we passed. Needless to say, he had fled, but his property and everything he possessed having been left behind, we were able, by confiscating them, to inflict some punishment for the immense amount of trouble he had brought on the credulous and easily-led tribesmen.

Many interesting curios, such as antiquated weapons and old books, were discovered by our men, usually hidden away in caves and holes in the hills. The Bunerwals, prior to our entering their country, had removed their goods and chattels to these places for security; their

UNIV. OF
CALIFORNIA

PIR BABA ZIARAT

women and cattle being also hidden away among the hills, where the former must have suffered great hardships from the intense cold.

By far the most picturesque spot which we saw in Buner was the Pir Baba ziarat.* Situated at the foot of a pine-clad range of hills, capped by a lofty snow-clad peak, and with a foreground of olive and Chenar trees throwing their shadows into the still depths of a pool beneath, the shrine of this much-revered saint had certainly been erected among pleasant surroundings. Here our Mohammedan sepoys offered up their petitions; no one, except those of this faith, being allowed to enter the sacred precincts. It was, indeed, a strange sight to see our men, clad in uniform, side by side with the tribesmen, all thoughts of war laid aside, as both victor and vanquished paid their devotions together.

Thus our campaign ended; as, marching out through the Chamla Valley, where the

* Burial-place.

Government terms were at once submitted to, we passed over the border into Indian territory on the 18th January, crossing the range of hills by the Ambéla Pass.

Here, on either side of the crest tower, were the rocky heights known as the Crag Piquet and Eagle's Rest, scenes of much hard fighting during Sir Neville Chamberlain's advance into Chamla to punish the Hindustani fanatics, and passing these places where the marks of the old defences still remained, our thoughts went back to that period when the 71st Highlanders, now known as the 1st Battalion Highland Light Infantry, fought so well, retaking the Crag after it had been captured by the enemy. Now, after a space of thirty-four years, their 2nd Battalion were marching over the same ground, with pipes playing their tribute to the memory of the many gallant officers and men of the regiment who lost their lives on that occasion.

CHAPTER XVII

A RETROSPECT—THE BUNERWALS—MANNERS AND CUSTOMS—"WESH"

TWO other regiments now forming part of our force had also fought among these hills under General Chamberlain, the Guides and 20th Punjab Infantry, the former of these being the regiment selected at the end of that campaign to proceed to Malka, the headquarters of the Hindustani fanatics, who were the primary cause and objective of the expedition.

Malka was too far down the Chamla Valley for us to see it, and there is probably little left of it now, having been burnt by the Guides on the above-mentioned occasion; aided in this work by the Bunerwals, who, after the defeat of the tribal gathering on the Ambéla Pass, not only tendered their submission, but offered to destroy the settlement and disperse the colony of their late allies.

History repeats itself. For, during the present expedition, the Hindustani fanatics, who partook with the Bunerwals in the defence of their passes, were, on the submission of the latter, again driven to take refuge in a more remote portion of the country; the tribesmen fearing lest the gathering which these fanatics were raising to oppose our advance would cause retribution to fall on their own heads.

An old man who accompanied us up the pass had formerly, we discovered, served as a native officer in the 20th P.I., and having taken part in the Ambéla campaign, was able to point out all the old positions, giving at the same time many interesting details of the various fights.

The pass itself is not a hard one; the gradients of the ascent being far easier than those of the passes leading immediately into Buner. But the difficulties the troops had to contend with were doubtless somewhat increased by the dense jungle which covers these hills, and out of which the rocky knoll, known as the Crag Piquet, rises. Climbing up to examine this spot, all the traces we could discover of that past campaign were some broken beer bottles, the only relic of a bygone British occupation.

Although the most peaceful of the frontier tribes, the Bunerwals are looked up to and respected by their neighbours for many soldierly qualities, and they are supposed to be the best swordsmen on the border. Although excessively under the influence of their Mullahs, they have given us little trouble, and among themselves, from what we saw of their villages, unfortified and built in the open, they evidently live more at peace than is usual among Pathans.

Blood feuds exist; but this method of settling disputes is a particularly effective form of administering justice amongst a wild and uncivilised people, to whom the complicated and lengthy procedure of our law courts would necessarily be ill-suited.

These blood feuds, which can often be settled by payment of a sum of money, fixed on by one of their Mullahs or other intermediary, arise, as a rule, from a breach of the seventh commandment. In such a case the injured husband either kills his wife or mutilates her by cutting her nose off, and turning her out of the house. It is incumbent on him, in addition to this, to pursue relentlessly the man who caused the conjugal difficulty until he succeeds in killing him, otherwise, he lays himself open to a blood feud with his wife's relations, in which he is pretty certain to be killed himself.

On the other hand, if having killed the latter, he deems his revenge satisfied and refrains from chastising his wife, he is at once involved in a blood feud with the man's relatives.

A call to arms is a constant feature of life in these rugged highlands: in fact, the tenure of a great portion of the arable land is based on a feudal system, under which the tenant is bound to turn out with his matchlock or rifle, and, with a skin of flour on his back, fight perhaps for days at a time in pursuance of the quarrels of his feudal superior.

"Wesh" is still practised by most sections of the Bunerwals and Swatis: this peculiar custom being the redistribution of land by lot every ten years. The arguments in favour of such an arrangement are difficult to find, and as in the carrying out it is almost always the cause of quarrels and bloodshed, it is apparently by no means popular with the people.

The Bunerwals have a good reputation, and they are doubtless superior to their neighbours in some respects, being free from many of the baser qualities of the Pathan. Like the Swatis, they do not sell their wives, this being a common practice among the Utman Khel and Bajour people, who either sell or exchange their women for rifles. On the other hand, they are the most ignorant and priest-ridden of the tribes, poor and unable, owing to their contempt for trade, to avail themselves of the rich income which goes entirely to the Hindus on our side of the border. These latter amass great wealth by sending their agents into the principal villages, and exporting the produce of the country, principally rice and ghi, the rice being of a peculiarly good quality and highly valued.

One effect of the punitive expeditions of 1897-98 have been to largely increase our knowledge of the countries touching our North-West frontier. Buner is almost the last of the unknown lands, and has proved in many ways very different to the ideas which, derived from native sources, have proved most unreliable. It seems strange that a country co-terminous with British territory for some years past should be practically unknown, and the Government survey, which was carried out under

Captain Robertson, R.E., during our march through the country, should considerably alter the existing maps of these regions.

Our operations altogether embraced a large portion of unsurveyed country, populated by tribes for whose actions, being situated on this side of the Durand boundary line, we are to some extent responsible. For however shadowy our influence up to that boundary may be, the fact of its being demarcated declared all tribes on this side as being within our sphere of influence. If these tribes were able to refrain from trespassing on British territory, raiding villages under British rule, there would be no need for interference; but such a race will never be able to remain within their own limits: their latent fanaticism is either aroused by their religious leaders, or, like children, they are led away by the excitement of the moment, joining in some raid or otherwise committing themselves against the Government.

This has led to the construction of posts

beyond our frontier in order to prevent incursions of the tribes into British territory, but it is difficult with such a people to maintain such a firm hold on them as to prevent disturbances and at the same time not interfere with their tribal affairs.

Thus the frontier remains a source of perpetual joy to the soldier, but to the politician a problem yet to be solved.

The orders for the demobilisation of our troops arrived on the 21st of January, Sir Bindon Blood's farewell address being published in the Field Force Orders as follows:—

"Orders have been received for the immediate break-up of the Buner Field Force. Major-General Sir Bindon Blood, K.C.B., has to take leave of the troops he has commanded with pride and satisfaction for nearly six months in the field. The Malakand Field Force, which the Major-General joined on the 31st July 1897, and which ceased to exist as a Field Force on the 7th instant, was actively employed for three and a half months in marching and fighting, some of the fighting being of a most severe and difficult character. During this time much was achieved, and the conduct and bearing of all ranks was uniformly such as to prove their high character as soldiers, as well as earn the warmly-expressed approval of the highest authorities. The Buner Field Force has only been in existence fifteen days, but during that time it has finally laid the 'spectre of Ambéla.' Sir Bindon Blood wishes a cordial farewell to all who have served under his command in the Malakand and Buner Field Forces."

END

LIST OF OFFICERS KILLED AND WOUNDED

Name.	Place.	Date.	
Lieut. L. Manley, Commissariat Department	Malakand	26/7/97	Killed
Major W. W. Taylor, 45th Sikhs	,,	,,	,,
Lieut.-Col. J. Lamb, 24th Punjab Infantry	,,	,,	Died of wounds
Major L. Herbert, C.I.H., D.A.A.G.	,,	,,	Wounded
Captain F. Holland, 24th Punjab Infantry	,,	,,	,,
Lieut. F. W. Watling, Q.O. Sappers & Miners	,,	,,	,,
Lieut. E. W. Costello, 24th Punjab Infantry	,,	27/7/97	Twice wounded
Lieut. H. L. S. Maclean, Guides Cavalry	,,	28/7/97	,, Afterwards killed at Landakai 17/8/97
Lieut. H. B. Ford, 31st Punjab Infantry	,,	,,	Wounded

APPENDIX

Name.	Place.	Date.	
Lieut. G. D. Swinley, 31st Punjab Infantry	Malakand	28/7/97	Wounded
Lieut. G. M. Baldwin, Guides Cavalry	,,	1/8/97	,,
Lieut. C. V. Keyes, Guides Cavalry	,,	,,	,,
Lieut. F. A. Wynter, Royal Artillery	,,	30/7/97	,,
Lieut. H. B. Rattray, 45th Sikhs	Chakdara	2/8/97	,,
Lieut. R. T. Greaves, Lancashire Fusiliers	Landakai	17/8/97	Killed
Captain H. I. E. Palmer, 5th Punjab Cavalry	,,	,,	Wounded
Captain W. E. Tomkins, 38th Dogras	Markhanai	14/9/97	Killed
Lieut. A. W. Bailey, 38th Dogras	,,	,,	,,
Lieut. C. D. M. Harrington, 38th Dogras	,,	,,	Died of wounds
Lieut. V. Hughes, 35th Sikhs	Shahi Tangi	16/9/97	Killed
Lieut. A. T. Crawford, Royal Artillery	,,	,,	,,

APPENDIX

Lieut. O. G. Gunning, 35th Sikhs	Shahi Tangi	16/9/97	Wounded
Captain W. J. Ryder, 35th Sikhs	,,	,,	,,
Lieut. G. R. Cassels, 35th Sikhs	,,	,,	,,
Lieut. T. C. Watson, R.E.	Bilot	,,	,,
Lieut. F. A. Wynter, Royal Artillery	,,	,,	,,
2nd Lieut. G. N. S. Keene, unattached List	Lagai	21/9/97	,,
Lieut. R. E. Power, Buffs	,,	,,	,,
Major R. S. H. Moody, Buffs	Tangi	23/9/97	,,
Lieut.-Col. J. L. O'Bryen, 31st Punjab Infantry	Agrah and Gat	30/9/97	Killed
2nd Lieut. W. C. Browne Clayton, R. W. Kent	,,	,,	,,
Lieut. H. Isacke, R. W. Kent	,,	,,	Wounded
Major Western, R. W. Kent	,,	,,	,,
Captain R. C. Style, R. W. Kent	,,	,,	,,
Captain N. H. S. Low, R. W. Kent	,,	,,	,,
2nd Lieut. F. A. Jackson, R. W. Kent	,,	,,	,,

Name.	Place.	Date.	
Lieut. E. B. Peacock, 31st Punjab Infantry	Agrah and Gat	30/9/97	Wounded
Brigadier-General I. Wodehouse, C.B.	Nawagai	20/9/97	,,
Veterinary-Captain Mann, A.V.D.	,,	,,	,,
Captain L. I. B. Hulke, Buffs	Lagai	21/9/97	,,

A CATALOGUE OF BOOKS AND ANNOUNCEMENTS OF METHUEN AND COMPANY PUBLISHERS : LONDON 36 ESSEX STREET W.C.

CONTENTS

	PAGE
FORTHCOMING BOOKS,	2
POETRY,	8
BELLES LETTRES, ANTHOLOGIES, ETC.,	9
ILLUSRTATED BOOKS,	10
HISTORY,	11
BIOGRAPHY,	14
TRAVEL, ADVENTURE AND TOPOGRAPHY,	15
NAVAL AND MILITARY,	17
GENERAL LITERATURE,	18
SCIENCE AND TECHNOLOGY,	20
PHILOSOPHY,	20
THEOLOGY,	21
FICTION,	24
BOOKS FOR BOYS AND GIRLS,	34
THE PEACOCK LIBRARY,	34
UNIVERSITY EXTENSION SERIES,	35
SOCIAL QUESTIONS OF TO-DAY	36
CLASSICAL TRANSLATIONS	37
EDUCATIONAL BOOKS,	37

DECEMBER 1898

DECEMBER 1898

MESSRS. METHUEN'S
ANNOUNCEMENTS

Travel and Adventure

NORTHWARD: OVER THE GREAT ICE. By R. E. PEARY. With over 800 Illustrations, Maps and Diagrams. *Two Volumes. Royal 8vo. 32s. net.*

In this important work Lieutenant Peary tells the story of his travels and adventures in the Arctic regions. His extraordinary sledge journey and his experience among the Eskimos are fully described, and this book is a complete record of his Arctic work, for which the Royal Geographical Society has this year awarded him their Gold Medal.

The fact that Lieutenant Peary is about to start on a determined effort to reach the North Pole lends a special interest to this book.

THROUGH ASIA. By SVEN HEDIN. With over 250 Illustrations from Sketches and Photographs by the Author, and 6 Maps. *Two volumes. Royal 8vo. 36s. net.*

In this book Dr. Sven Hedin, the distinguished Swedish explorer, describes his four years' experiences and his extraordinary adventures in Central Asia. Dr. Hedin is an accomplished artist, and his drawings are full of vigour and interest.

In adventurous interest and substantial results in various departments of knowledge, Dr. Hedin's journey will bear comparison with the travels of the great explorers of the past, from Marco Polo downwards.

The Gold Medals of the Royal Geographical Society and of the Russian Geographical Society have been conferred upon him for this journey.

THE HIGHEST ANDES. By E. A. FITZGERALD. With 40 Illustrations, 10 of which are Photogravures, and a Large Map. *Royal 8vo. 30s. net.*

Also, a Small Edition on Handmade Paper, limited to 50 Copies, *4to. £5, 5s.*

A narrative of the highest climb yet accomplished. The illustrations have been reproduced with the greatest care, and the book, in addition to its adventurous interest, contains appendices of great scientific value.

CHITRAL: The Story of a Minor Siege. By SIR G. S. ROBERTSON, K.C.S.I. With Numerous Illustrations and a Map. *Demy 8vo. 21s. net.*

Sir George Robertson, who was at the time British Agent at Gilgit, has written the story of Chitral from the point of view of one actually besieged in the fort. The book is of considerable length, and has an Introductory part explaining the series of events which culminated in the famous siege; also an account of Ross's disaster in the KORAGH defile, the heroic defence of RESHUN, and Kelly's great march. It has numerous illustrations—plans, pictures and portraits—and a map, and will give a connected narrative of the stirring episodes on the Chitral frontier in 1895.

TWENTY YEARS IN THE NEAR EAST. By A. HULME
BEAMAN. With Portrait. *Demy 8vo.* 10s. 6d.

> A personal narrative of experiences in Syria, Egypt, Turkey and the Balkan States, including adventures in the Lebanon, during the bombardment of Alexandra, the first Egyptian Campaign, the Dongola Expedition, the Cretan Insurrection, etc. The book also contains several chapters on Turkey, its people and its Sultan.

THE DOWNFALL OF THE DERVISHES: BEING A SKETCH OF THE FINAL SUDAN CAMPAIGN OF 1898. By ERNEST N. BENNETT, M.A., Fellow and Lecturer of Hertford College, Oxford; Special Correspondent for *The Westminster Gazette*. With a Photogravure Portrait of the Sirdar, a Map, and Two Plans. *Crown 8vo.* 3s. 6d.

Theology

DOCTRINE AND DEVELOPMENT. By HASTINGS RASHDALL, M.A., Fellow and Tutor of New College, Oxford. *Crown 8vo.* 6s.

> This volume consists of twenty sermons, preached chiefly before the University of Oxford. They are an attempt to translate into the language of modern thought some of the leading ideas of Christian theology and ethics.

CLOVELLY SERMONS. By WILLIAM HARRISON, M.A., late Rector of Clovelly. With a Preface by LUCAS MALET. *Crown 8vo.* 3s. 6d.

> A volume of Sermons by a son-in-law of Charles Kingsley.

APOSTOLIC CHRISTIANITY: As Illustrated by the Epistles of S. Paul to the Corinthians. By H. H. HENSON, M.A., Fellow of All Souls', Oxford. *Crown 8vo.* 6s.

Handbooks of Theology.
General Editor, A. ROBERTSON, D.D., Principal of King's College, London.

THE XXXIX. ARTICLES OF THE CHURCH OF ENGLAND. Edited with an Introduction by E. C. S. GIBSON, D.D., Vicar of Leeds, late Principal of Wells Theological College. *Revised and Cheaper Edition in One Volume. Demy 8vo.* 12s. 6d.

AN INTRODUCTION TO THE HISTORY OF THE CREEDS. By A. E. BURN, Examining Chaplain to the Bishop of Lichfield. *Demy 8vo.* 10s. 6d.

The Churchman's Library.
Edited by J. H. BURN, B.D.

A series of books by competent scholars on Church History, Institutions, and Doctrine, for the use of clerical and lay readers.

THE KINGDOM OF HEAVEN HERE AND HEREAFTER. By Canon WINTERBOTHAM, M.A., B.Sc., LL.B. *Crown 8vo.* 3s. 6d.

Oxford Commentaries.

General Editor, WALTER LOCK, D.D., Warden of Keble College, Dean Ireland's Professor of Exegesis in the University of Oxford.

Messrs. METHUEN propose to issue a series of Commentaries upon such Books of the Bible as still seem to need further explanation.

The object of each Commentary is primarily exegetical, to interpret the author's meaning to the present generation. The editors will not deal, except very subordinately, with questions of textual criticism or philology; but taking the English text in the Revised Version as their basis, they will try to combine a hearty acceptance of critical principles with loyalty to the Catholic Faith. It is hoped that in this way the series may be of use both to theological students and to the clergy, and also to the growing number of educated laymen and laywomen who wish to read the Bible intelligently and reverently.

THE BOOK OF JOB. Edited, with Introduction and Notes, by E. C. S. GIBSON, D.D., Vicar of Leeds. *Demy 8vo.* 6s.

The Library of Devotion.

Pott 8vo, cloth, 2s.; leather, 2s. 6d. net.

NEW VOLUMES.

A SERIOUS CALL TO A DEVOUT AND HOLY LIFE. By WILLIAM LAW. Edited, with an Introduction, Analysis, and Notes, by C. BIGG, D.D.

A BOOK OF DEVOTIONS. By J. W. STANBRIDGE, M.A., Rector of Bainton, Canon of York, and sometime Fellow of S^t. John's College, Oxford.

This book contains devotions, Eucharistic, daily and occasional, for the use of members of the English Church, sufficiently diversified for those who possess other works of the kind. It is intended to be a companion in private and public worship, and is in harmony with the thoughts of the best Devotional writers.

History and Biography

MEMOIRS OF ADMIRAL THE RIGHT HONBLE. SIR ASTLEY COOPER KEY. By Vice-Admiral P. H. COLOMB. With Portrait. *Demy 8vo.* 16s.

This life of a great sailor throws a considerable light on the evolution of the Navy during the last fifty years.

THE DECLINE AND FALL OF THE ROMAN EMPIRE. By EDWARD GIBBON. A New Edition, edited with Notes, Appendices, and Maps by J. B. BURY, LL.D., Fellow of Trinity College, Dublin. *In Seven Volumes. Demy 8vo, gilt top.* 8s. 6d. each. *Crown 8vo.* 6s. each. *Vol. VI.*

A HISTORY OF EGYPT, FROM THE EARLIEST TIMES TO THE PRESENT DAY. Edited by W. M. FLINDERS PETRIE, D.C.L., LL.D., Professor of Egyptology at University College. *Fully Illustrated. In Six Volumes. Crown 8vo. 6s. each.*

Vol. IV. THE EGYPT OF THE PTOLEMIES. J. P. MAHAFFY.

Vol. V. ROMAN EGYPT. J. G. MILNE.

THE CANON LAW IN ENGLAND. By F. W. MAITLAND, LL.D., Downing Professor of the Laws of England in the University of Cambridge. *Royal 8vo. 7s. 6d.*

  A volume of Essays on the History of the Canon Law in England. These Essays deal chiefly with the measure of authority attributed in medieval England to the papal law-books, and one entitled (1) *William Lyndwood*, (2) *Church, State and Decretals*, (3) *William of Drogheda and the Universal Ordinary*, (4) *Henry II. and the Criminous Clerks*, (5) *Execrabilis in the Common Pleas*, and (6) *The Deacon and the Jewess*.

ANNALS OF SHREWSBURY SCHOOL. By G. W. FISHER, M.A., Assistant Master. With Numerous Illustrations. *Demy 8vo. 10s. 6d.*

ANNALS OF WESTMINSTER SCHOOL. By J. SARGEAUNT, M.A., Assistant Master. With Numerous Illustrations. *Demy 8vo. 7s. 6d.*

ANNALS OF ETON COLLEGE. By W. STERRY, M.A. With Numerous Illustrations. *Demy 8vo. 7s. 6d.*

General Literature

THE PILGRIM'S PROGRESS. By JOHN BUNYAN. Edited, with an Introduction, by C. H. FIRTH, M.A. With 39 Illustrations by R. ANNING BELL. *Crown 8vo. 6s.*

  This book contains a long Introduction by Mr. Firth, whose knowledge of the period is unrivalled; and it is lavishly illustrated.

AN OLD ENGLISH HOME. By S. BARING GOULD. With Numerous Plans and Illustrations. *Crown 8vo. 6s.*

  This book describes the life and environment of an old English family.

CAMBRIDGE AND ITS COLLEGES. By A. HAMILTON THOMPSON. With Illustrations by E. H. NEW. *Pott 8vo. Cloth, 3s. Leather, 4s.*

  This book is uniform with Mr. Wells's very successful book, 'Oxford and its Colleges.'

UNIVERSITY AND SOCIAL SETTLEMENTS. By W. REASON, M.A. *Crown 8vo. 2s. 6d.* [*Social Question Series.*

DANTE'S GARDEN. By ROSEMARY COTES. With a frontispiece *Fcap. 8vo. 2s. 6d.*

  An account of the flowers mentioned by Dante, with their legends.

READING AND READERS. By CLIFFORD HARRISON. *Fcap. 8vo. 2s. 6d.*

  A little book of principles and hints by the most distinguished of living reciters.

VENTURES IN VERSE. By B. J. WILLIAMS. *Cr. 8vo. 3s. 6d.*

Educational

VOLUMETRIC ANALYSIS. By J. B. RUSSELL, B.Sc., Science Master at Burnley Grammar School. *Crown 8vo.* 1s.

A small Manual, containing all the necessary rules, etc., on a subject which has hitherto only been treated in expensive volumes.

A KEY TO STEDMAN'S EASY FRENCH EXERCISES. By G. A. SCHRUMPF. *Crown 8vo.* 3s. net.

A SHORTER GREEK PRIMER. By A. M. M. STEDMAN, M.A. *Crown 8vo.* 1s. 6d.

A book which contains the elements of Accidence and Syntax.

CARPENTRY AND JOINERY. By F. C. WEBBER. With many Illustrations. *Crown 8vo.* 3s. 6d.
 [*Text-books of Technology.*

A Manual for technical classes and self-instruction.

PRACTICAL MECHANICS. By SIDNEY H. WELLS. Illustrated. *Crown 8vo.* 3s. 6d. [*Text-books of Technology.*

A CLASS-BOOK OF DICTATION PASSAGES. By W. WILLIAMSON, M.A. *Crown 8vo.* 1s. 6d.

The passages are culled from recognised authors, and a few newspaper passages are included. The lists of appended words are drawn up mainly on the principle of comparison and contrast, and will form a repertoire of over 2000 words, embracing practically all the difficulties felt by the pupil.

AN ENTRANCE GUIDE TO THE PROFESSIONS AND BUSINESS. By HENRY JONES. *Crown 8vo.* 1s. 6d.
 [*Commercial Series.*

Byzantine Texts

Edited by J. B. BURY, LL.D., Professor of Modern History at Trinity College, Dublin.

EVAGRIUS. Edited by PROFESSOR LÉON PARMENTIER of Liége and M. BIDEZ of Gand. *Demy 8vo.*

Cheaper Editions

BRITISH CENTRAL AFRICA. By Sir H. H. JOHNSTON, K.C.B. With nearly Two Hundred Illustrations, and Six Maps. *Revised and Cheaper Edition. Crown 4to.* 21s. net.

'The book is crowded with important information, and written in a most attractive style; it is worthy, in short, of the author's established reputation.'—*Standard.*

VAILIMA LETTERS. By ROBERT LOUIS STEVENSON. With an Etched Portrait by WILLIAM STRANG, and other Illustrations. *Cheaper Edition. Crown 8vo. Buckram.* 6s.

A BOOK OF CHRISTMAS VERSE. Edited by H. C. BEECHING, M.A., and Illustrated by WALTER CRANE. *Cheaper Edition. Crown 8vo, gilt top.* 3s. 6d.

A collection of the best verse inspired by the birth of Christ from the Middle Ages to the present day.

LYRA SACRA : An Anthology of Sacred Verse. Edited by H. C. BEECHING, M.A. *Cheaper Edition. Crown 8vo. Buckram.* 3s. 6d.
'A charming selection, which maintains a lofty standard of excellence.'—*Times.*

Fiction

THE BATTLE OF THE STRONG. By GILBERT PARKER, Author of 'The Seats of the Mighty.' *Crown 8vo.* 6s.
A romance of 1798.

THE TOWN TRAVELLER. By GEORGE GISSING, Author of 'Demos,' 'In the Year of Jubilee,' etc. *Crown 8vo.* 6s.

THE COUNTESS TEKLA. By ROBERT BARR, Author of 'The Mutable Many.' *Crown 8vo.* 6s.
A historical romance.

THINGS THAT HAVE HAPPENED. By DOROTHEA GERARD, Author of 'Lady Baby,' 'Orthodox,' etc. *Crown 8vo.* 6s.

DOMITIA. By S. BARING GOULD, Author of 'The Broom Squire,' etc. *Crown 8vo.* 6s.
A romance of imperial Rome.

FROM THE EAST UNTO THE WEST. By JANE BARLOW, Author of 'Irish Idylls,' 'A Creel of Irish Stories,' etc. *Crown 8vo.* 6s.

TO ARMS! By ANDREW BALFOUR, Author of 'By Stroke of Sword.' Illustrated. *Crown 8vo.* 6s.
A romance of 1715.

THE JOURNALIST. By C. F. KEARY. *Crown 8vo.* 6s.
A story of modern literary life.

PEGGY OF THE BARTONS. By B. M. CROKER, Author of 'Proper Pride.' *Crown 8vo.* 6s.

A VENDETTA OF THE DESERT. By W. C. SCULLY. *Crown 8vo.* 3s. 6d.
A South African romance.

CORRAGEEN IN '98. By Mrs. ORPEN. *Crown 8vo.* 6s.
A romance of the Irish Rebellion.

AN ENEMY TO THE KING. By R. N. STEPHENS. *Crown 8vo.* 6s.

THE PLUNDERPIT. By J. KEIGHLEY SNOWDEN. *Crown 8vo.* 6s.
A romance of adventure.

DEADMAN'S. By MARY GAUNT, Author of 'Kirkham's Find.' *Crown 8vo.* 6s.
An Australian story.

WILLOWBRAKE. By R. MURRAY GILCHRIST. *Crown 8vo.* 6s.

THE ANGEL OF THE COVENANT. By J. MACLAREN COBBAN. *Crown 8vo.* 6s.
A historical romance, of which Montrose is the hero.

OWD BOB, THE GREY DOG OF KENMUIR. By ALFRED OLLIVANT. *Crown 8vo.* 6s.
A story of the Cumberland dales.

ANANIAS. By the Hon. Mrs. ALAN BRODRICK. *Crown 8vo.* 6s.

ADVENTURES IN WALLYPUG LAND. By G. E. FARROW. With Illustrations by ALAN WRIGHT. *Crown 8vo. Gilt top.* 5s.

A LIST OF
MESSRS. METHUEN'S
PUBLICATIONS

Poetry

Rudyard Kipling. BARRACK-ROOM BALLADS. By RUDYARD KIPLING. *Fourteenth Edition. Crown 8vo. 6s.*

'Mr. Kipling's verse is strong, vivid, full of character. . . . Unmistakable genius rings in every line.'—*Times.*

'The ballads teem with imagination, they palpitate with emotion. We read them with laughter and tears; the metres throb in our pulses, the cunningly ordered words tingle with life; and if this be not poetry, what is?'—*Pall Mall Gazette.*

Rudyard Kipling. THE SEVEN SEAS. By RUDYARD KIPLING. *Fourth Edition. Crown 8vo. Buckram, gilt top. 6s.*

'The new poems of Mr. Rudyard Kipling have all the spirit and swing of their predecessors. Patriotism is the solid concrete foundation on which Mr. Kipling has built the whole of his work.'—*Times.*

'The Empire has found a singer; it is no depreciation of the songs to say that statesmen may have, one way or other, to take account of them.'—*Manchester Guardian.*

'Animated through and through with indubitable genius.'—*Daily Telegraph.*

"Q." POEMS AND BALLADS. By "Q." *Crown 8vo. 3s. 6d.*

'This work has just the faint, ineffable touch and glow that make poetry.'—*Speaker.*

"Q." GREEN BAYS: Verses and Parodies. By "Q.," Author of 'Dead Man's Rock,' etc. *Second Edition. Crown 8vo. 3s. 6d.*

E. Mackay. A SONG OF THE SEA. By ERIC MACKAY. *Second Edition. Fcap. 8vo. 5s.*

'Everywhere Mr. Mackay displays himself the master of a style marked by all the characteristics of the best rhetoric.'—*Globe.*

H. Ibsen. BRAND. A Drama by HENRIK IBSEN. Translated by WILLIAM WILSON. *Second Edition. Crown 8vo. 3s. 6d.*

'The greatest world-poem of the nineteenth century next to "Faust." It is in the same set with "Agamemnon," with "Lear," with the literature that we now instinctively regard as high and holy.'—*Daily Chronicle.*

"A. G." VERSES TO ORDER. By "A. G." *Cr. 8vo. 2s. 6d. net.*

'A capital specimen of light academic poetry.'—*St. James's Gazette.*

J. G. Cordery. THE ODYSSEY OF HOMER. A Translation by J. G. CORDERY. *Crown 8vo. 7s. 6d.*

Belles Lettres, Anthologies, etc.

R. L. Stevenson. VAILIMA LETTERS. By ROBERT LOUIS STEVENSON. With an Etched Portrait by WILLIAM STRANG, and other Illustrations. *Second Edition. Crown 8vo. Buckram. 6s.*

'A fascinating book.'—*Standard.*
'Full of charm and brightness.'—*Spectator.*
'A gift almost priceless.'—*Speaker.*
'Unique in literature.'—*Daily Chronicle.*

George Wyndham. THE POEMS OF WILLIAM SHAKESPEARE. Edited with an Introduction and Notes by GEORGE WYNDHAM, M.P. *Demy 8vo. Buckram, gilt top.* 10s. 6d.

This edition contains the 'Venus,' 'Lucrece,' and Sonnets, and is prefaced with an elaborate introduction of over 140 pp.

'One of the most serious contributions to Shakespearian criticism that has been published for some time.'—*Times.*
'One of the best pieces of editing in the language.'—*Outlook.*
'This is a scholarly and interesting contribution to Shakespearian literature.'—*Literature.*
'We have no hesitation in describing Mr. George Wyndham's introduction as a masterly piece of criticism, and all who love our Elizabethan literature will find a very garden of delight in it.'—*Spectator.*
'Mr. Wyndham's notes are admirable, even indispensable.'—*Westminster Gazette.*
'The standard edition of Shakespeare's poems.'—*World.*
'The book is written with critical insight and literary felicity.'—*Standard.*

W. E. Henley. ENGLISH LYRICS. Selected and Edited by W. E. HENLEY. *Crown 8vo. Buckram, gilt top. 6s.*

'It is a body of choice and lovely poetry.'—*Birmingham Gazette.*

Henley and Whibley. A BOOK OF ENGLISH PROSE. Collected by W. E. HENLEY and CHARLES WHIBLEY. *Crown 8vo. Buckram, gilt top. 6s.*

'Quite delightful. A greater treat for those not well acquainted with pre-Restoration prose could not be imagined.'—*Athenæum.*

H. C. Beeching. LYRA SACRA: An Anthology of Sacred Verse. Edited by H. C. BEECHING, M.A. *Crown 8vo. Buckram. 6s.*

'A charming selection, which maintains a lofty standard of excellence.'—*Times.*

"Q." THE GOLDEN POMP: A Procession of English Lyrics. Arranged by A. T. QUILLER COUCH. *Crown 8vo. Buckram. 6s.*

'A delightful volume: a really golden "Pomp."'—*Spectator.*

W. B. Yeats. AN ANTHOLOGY OF IRISH VERSE. Edited by W. B. YEATS. *Crown 8vo. 3s. 6d.*

'An attractive and catholic selection.'—*Times.*

G. W. Steevens. MONOLOGUES OF THE DEAD. By G. W. STEEVENS. *Foolscap 8vo. 3s. 6d.*

'The effect is sometimes splendid, sometimes bizarre, but always amazingly clever.'—*Pall Mall Gazette.*

W. M. Dixon. A PRIMER OF TENNYSON. By W. M. DIXON, M.A., Professor of English Literature at Mason College. *Crown 8vo. 2s. 6d.*

'Much sound and well-expressed criticism. The bibliography is a boon.'—*Speaker.*

W. A. Craigie. A PRIMER OF BURNS. By W. A. CRAIGIE. *Crown 8vo.* 2s. 6d.
'A valuable addition to the literature of the poet.'—*Times.*

L. Magnus. A PRIMER OF WORDSWORTH. By LAURIE MAGNUS. *Crown 8vo.* 2s. 6d.
'A valuable contribution to Wordsworthian literature.'—*Literature.*

Sterne. THE LIFE AND OPINIONS OF TRISTRAM SHANDY. By LAWRENCE STERNE. With an Introduction by CHARLES WHIBLEY, and a Portrait. 2 *vols.* 7s.
'Very dainty volumes are these; the paper, type, and light-green binding are all very agreeable to the eye.'—*Globe.*

Congreve. THE COMEDIES OF WILLIAM CONGREVE. With an Introduction by G. S. STREET, and a Portrait. 2 *vols.* 7s.

Morier. THE ADVENTURES OF HAJJI BABA OF ISPAHAN. By JAMES MORIER. With an Introduction by E. G. BROWNE, M.A., and a Portrait. 2 *vols.* 7s.

Walton. THE LIVES OF DONNE, WOTTON, HOOKER, HERBERT, AND SANDERSON. By IZAAK WALTON. With an Introduction by VERNON BLACKBURN, and a Portrait. 3s. 6d.

Johnson. THE LIVES OF THE ENGLISH POETS. By SAMUEL JOHNSON, LL.D. With an Introduction by J. H. MILLAR, and a Portrait. 3 *vols.* 10s. 6d.

Burns. THE POEMS OF ROBERT BURNS. Edited by ANDREW LANG and W. A. CRAIGIE. With Portrait. *Second Edition. Demy 8vo, gilt top.* 6s.
This edition contains a carefully collated Text, numerous Notes, critical and textual, a critical and biographical Introduction, and a Glossary.
'Among editions in one volume, this will take the place of authority.'—*Times.*

F. Langbridge. BALLADS OF THE BRAVE: Poems of Chivalry, Enterprise, Courage, and Constancy. Edited by Rev. F. LANGBRIDGE. *Second Edition. Crown 8vo.* 3s. 6d. *School Edition.* 2s. 6d.
'A very happy conception happily carried out. These "Ballads of the Brave" are intended to suit the real tastes of boys, and will suit the taste of the great majority.'—*Spectator.*   'The book is full of splendid things.'—*World.*

Illustrated Books

F. D. Bedford. NURSERY RHYMES. With many Coloured Pictures. By F. D. BEDFORD. *Super Royal 8vo.* 5s.
'An excellent selection of the best known rhymes, with beautifully coloured pictures exquisitely printed.'—*Pall Mall Gazette.*

S. Baring Gould. A BOOK OF FAIRY TALES retold by S. BARING GOULD. With numerous illustrations and initial letters by ARTHUR J. GASKIN. *Second Edition. Crown 8vo. Buckram.* 6s.
'Mr. Baring Gould is deserving of gratitude, in re-writing in simple style the old stories that delighted our fathers and grandfathers.'—*Saturday Review.*

S. Baring Gould. OLD ENGLISH FAIRY TALES. Collected and edited by S. BARING GOULD. With Numerous Illustrations by F. D. BEDFORD. *Second Edition. Crown 8vo. Buckram. 6s.*
'A charming volume. The stories have been selected with great ingenuity from various old ballads and folk-tales, and now stand forth, clothed in Mr. Baring Gould's delightful English, to enchant youthful readers.'—*Guardian.*

S. Baring Gould. A BOOK OF NURSERY SONGS AND RHYMES. Edited by S. BARING GOULD, and Illustrated by the Birmingham Art School. *Buckram, gilt top. Crown 8vo. 6s.*
'The volume is very complete in its way, as it contains nursery songs to the number of 77, game-rhymes, and jingles. To the student we commend the sensible introduction, and the explanatory notes.'—*Birmingham Gazette.*

H. C. Beeching. A BOOK OF CHRISTMAS VERSE. Edited by H. C. BEECHING, M.A., and Illustrated by WALTER CRANE. *Crown 8vo, gilt top. 5s.*
An anthology which, from its unity of aim and high poetic excellence, has a better right to exist than most of its fellows.'—*Guardian.*

History

Gibbon. THE DECLINE AND FALL OF THE ROMAN EMPIRE. By EDWARD GIBBON. A New Edition, Edited with Notes, Appendices, and Maps, by J. B. BURY, LL.D., Fellow of Trinity College, Dublin. *In Seven Volumes. Demy 8vo. Gilt top. 8s. 6d. each. Also crown 8vo. 6s. each. Vols. I., II., III., IV., and V.*

'The time has certainly arrived for a new edition of Gibbon's great work. . . . Professor Bury is the right man to undertake this task. His learning is amazing, both in extent and accuracy. The book is issued in a handy form, and at a moderate price, and it is admirably printed.'—*Times.*
'This edition, is a marvel of erudition and critical skill, and it is the very minimum of praise to predict that the seven volumes of it will supersede Dean Milman's as the standard edition of our great historical classic.'—*Glasgow Herald.*
'At last there is an adequate modern edition of Gibbon. . . . The best edition the nineteenth century could produce.'—*Manchester Guardian.*

Flinders Petrie. A HISTORY OF EGYPT, FROM THE EARLIEST TIMES TO THE PRESENT DAY. Edited by W. M. FLINDERS PETRIE, D.C.L., LL.D., Professor of Egyptology at University College. *Fully Illustrated. In Six Volumes. Crown 8vo. 6s. each.*

    Vol. I. PREHISTORIC TIMES TO XVITH DYNASTY. W. M. F. Petrie. *Third Edition.*
    Vol. II. THE XVIITH AND XVIIITH DYNASTIES. W. M. F. Petrie. *Second Edition.*

'A history written in the spirit of scientific precision so worthily represented by Dr. Petrie and his school cannot but promote sound and accurate study, and supply a vacant place in the English literature of Egyptology.'—*Times.*

Flinders Petrie. RELIGION AND CONSCIENCE IN ANCIENT EGYPT. By W. M. FLINDERS PETRIE, D.C.L., LL.D. Fully Illustrated. *Crown 8vo. 2s. 6d.*
'The lectures will afford a fund of valuable information for students of ancient ethics.—*Manchester Guardian.*

Flinders Petrie. SYRIA AND EGYPT, FROM THE TELL EL AMARNA TABLETS. By W. M. FLINDERS PETRIE, D.C.L., LL.D. *Crown 8vo.* 2s. 6d.

'A marvellous record. The addition made to our knowledge is nothing short of amazing.'—*Times.*

Flinders Petrie. EGYPTIAN TALES. Edited by W. M. FLINDERS PETRIE. Illustrated by TRISTRAM ELLIS. *In Two Volumes. Crown 8vo.* 3s. 6d. each.

'A valuable addition to the literature of comparative folk-lore. The drawings are really illustrations in the literal sense of the word.'—*Globe.*
'Invaluable as a picture of life in Palestine and Egypt.'—*Daily News.*

Flinders Petrie. EGYPTIAN DECORATIVE ART. By W. M. FLINDERS PETRIE. With 120 Illustrations. *Cr. 8vo.* 3s. 6d.

'In these lectures he displays rare skill in elucidating the development of decorative art in Egypt, and in tracing its influence on the art of other countries.'—*Times.*

C. W. Oman. A HISTORY OF THE ART OF WAR. Vol. II.: The Middle Ages, from the Fourth to the Fourteenth Century. By C. W. OMAN, M.A., Fellow of All Souls', Oxford. Illustrated. *Demy 8vo.* 21s.

'The book is based throughout upon a thorough study of the original sources, and will be an indispensable aid to all students of mediæval history.'—*Athenæum.*
'The whole art of war in its historic evolution has never been treated on such an ample and comprehensive scale, and we question if any recent contribution to the exact history of the world has possessed greater and more enduring value.'—*Daily Chronicle.*

S. Baring Gould. THE TRAGEDY OF THE CÆSARS. With numerous Illustrations from Busts, Gems, Cameos, etc. By S. BARING GOULD. *Fourth Edition. Royal 8vo.* 15s.

'A most splendid and fascinating book on a subject of undying interest. The great feature of the book is the use the author has made of the existing portraits of the Caesars, and the admirable critical subtlety he has exhibited in dealing with this line of research. It is brilliantly written, and the illustrations are supplied on a scale of profuse magnificence.'—*Daily Chronicle.*

H. de B. Gibbins. INDUSTRY IN ENGLAND: HISTORICAL OUTLINES. By H. DE B. GIBBINS, M.A., D.Litt. With 5 Maps. *Second Edition. Demy 8vo.* 10s. 6d.

H. E. Egerton. A HISTORY OF BRITISH COLONIAL POLICY. By H. E. EGERTON, M.A. *Demy 8vo.* 12s. 6d.

'It is a good book, distinguished by accuracy in detail, clear arrangement of facts, and a broad grasp of principles.'—*Manchester Guardian.*
'Able, impartial, clear. . . . A most valuable volume.'—*Athenæum.*

Albert Sorel. THE EASTERN QUESTION IN THE EIGHTEENTH CENTURY. By ALBERT SOREL, of the French Academy. Translated by F. C. BRAMWELL, M.A., with an Introduction by R. C. L. FLETCHER, Fellow of Magdalen College, Oxford. With a Map. *Crown 8vo.* 4s. 6d.

'The author's insight into the character and motives of the leading actors in the drama gives the work an interest uncommon in books based on similar material.'—*Scotsman.*

C. H. Grinling. A HISTORY OF THE GREAT NORTHERN RAILWAY, 1845-95. By CHARLES H. GRINLING. With Maps and Illustrations. *Demy 8vo.* 10s. 6d.

'Admirably written, and crammed with interesting facts.'—*Daily Mail.*
'The only adequate history of a great English railway company that has as yet appeared.'—*Times.*
'Mr. Grinling has done for the history of the Great Northern what Macaulay did for English History.'—*The Engineer.*

A. Clark. THE COLLEGES OF OXFORD: Their History and their Traditions. By Members of the University. Edited by A. CLARK, M.A., Fellow and Tutor of Lincoln College. *8vo.* 12s. 6d.

'A work which will certainly be appealed to for many years as the standard book on the Colleges of Oxford.'—*Athenæum.*

Perrens. THE HISTORY OF FLORENCE FROM 1434 TO 1492. By F. T. PERRENS. *8vo.* 12s. 6d.

A history of Florence under the domination of Cosimo, Piero, and Lorenzo de Medicis.

J. Wells. A SHORT HISTORY OF ROME. By J. WELLS, M.A., Fellow and Tutor of Wadham Coll., Oxford. With 4 Maps. *Second Edition. Crown 8vo.* 3s. 6d.

This book is intended for the Middle and Upper Forms of Public Schools and for Pass Students at the Universities. It contains copious Tables, etc.
'An original work written on an original plan, and with uncommon freshness and vigour.'—*Speaker.*

O. Browning. A SHORT HISTORY OF MEDIÆVAL ITALY, A.D. 1250-1530. By OSCAR BROWNING, Fellow and Tutor of King's College, Cambridge. *Second Edition. In Two Volumes. Crown 8vo.* 5s. each.

VOL. I. 1250-1409.—Guelphs and Ghibellines.
VOL. II. 1409-1530.—The Age of the Condottieri.

'Mr. Browning is to be congratulated on the production of a work of immense labour and learning.'—*Westminster Gazette.*

O'Grady. THE STORY OF IRELAND. By STANDISH O'GRADY, Author of 'Finn and his Companions.' *Cr. 8vo.* 2s. 6d.

'Most delightful, most stimulating. Its racy humour, its original imaginings, make it one of the freshest, breeziest volumes.'—*Methodist Times.*

Biography

S. Baring Gould. THE LIFE OF NAPOLEON BONAPARTE. By S. BARING GOULD. With over 450 Illustrations in the Text and 12 Photogravure Plates. *Large quarto. Gilt top.* 36s.

> 'The best biography of Napoleon in our tongue, nor have the French as good a biographer of their hero. A book very nearly as good as Southey's "Life of Nelson."'—*Manchester Guardian.*
>
> 'The main feature of this gorgeous volume is its great wealth of beautiful photogravures and finely-executed wood engravings, constituting a complete pictorial chronicle of Napoleon I.'s personal history from the days of his early childhood at Ajaccio to the date of his second interment.'—*Daily Telegraph.*
>
> 'Nearly all the illustrations are real contributions to history.'—*Westminster Gazette.*

Morris Fuller. THE LIFE AND WRITINGS OF JOHN DAVENANT, D.D. (1571-1641), Bishop of Salisbury. By MORRIS FULLER, B.D. *Demy 8vo.* 10s. 6d.

J. M. Rigg. ST. ANSELM OF CANTERBURY: A CHAPTER IN THE HISTORY OF RELIGION. By J. M. RIGG. *Demy 8vo.* 7s. 6d.

> 'Mr. Rigg has told the story of the life with scholarly ability, and has contributed an interesting chapter to the history of the Norman period.'—*Daily Chronicle.*

F. W. Joyce. THE LIFE OF SIR FREDERICK GORE OUSELEY. By F. W. JOYCE, M.A. 7s. 6d.

> 'This book has been undertaken in quite the right spirit, and written with sympathy, insight, and considerable literary skill.'—*Times.*

W. G. Collingwood. THE LIFE OF JOHN RUSKIN. By W. G. COLLINGWOOD, M.A. With Portraits, and 13 Drawings by Mr. Ruskin. *Second Edition.* 2 vols. *8vo.* 32s.

> 'No more magnificent volumes have been published for a long time.'—*Times.*
>
> 'It is long since we had a biography with such delights of substance and of form. Such a book is a pleasure for the day, and a joy for ever.'—*Daily Chronicle.*

C. Waldstein. JOHN RUSKIN. By CHARLES WALDSTEIN, M.A. With a Photogravure Portrait. *Post 8vo.* 5s.

> 'A thoughtful and well-written criticism of Ruskin's teaching.'—*Daily Chronicle.*

A. M. F. Darmesteter. THE LIFE OF ERNEST RENAN. By MADAME DARMESTETER. With Portrait. *Second Edition. Cr. 8vo.* 6s.

> 'A polished gem of biography, superior in its kind to any attempt that has been made of recent years in England. Madame Darmesteter has indeed written for English readers "The Life of Ernest Renan."'—*Athenæum.*
>
> 'It is a fascinating and biographical and critical study, and an admirably finished work of literary art.'—*Scotsman.*
>
> 'It is interpenetrated with the dignity and charm, the mild, bright, classical grace of form and treatment that Renan himself so loved; and it fulfils to the uttermost the delicate and difficult achievement it sets out to accomplish.'—*Academy.*

W. H. Hutton. THE LIFE OF SIR THOMAS MORE. By W. H. HUTTON, M.A. *With Portraits. Crown 8vo.* 5s.

> 'The book lays good claim to high rank among our biographies. It is excellently, even lovingly, written.'—*Scotsman.*   'An excellent monograph.'—*Times.*

Travel, Adventure and Topography

H. H. Johnston. BRITISH CENTRAL AFRICA. By Sir H. H. JOHNSTON, K.C.B. With nearly Two Hundred Illustrations, and Six Maps. *Second Edition. Crown 4to. 30s. net.*

'A fascinating book, written with equal skill and charm—the work at once of a literary artist and of a man of action who is singularly wise, brave, and experienced. It abounds in admirable sketches from pencil.'—*Westminster Gazette.*

'A delightful book . . . collecting within the covers of a single volume all that is known of this part of our African domains. The voluminous appendices are of extreme value.'—*Manchester Guardian.*

'The book takes front rank as a standard work by the one man competent to write it.'—*Daily Chronicle.*

L. Decle. THREE YEARS IN SAVAGE AFRICA. By LIONEL DECLE. With 100 Illustrations and 5 Maps. *Second Edition. Demy 8vo. 21s.*

'A fine, full book.'—*Pall Mall Gazette.*
'Abounding in thrilling adventures.'—*Daily Telegraph.*
'His book is profusely illustrated, and its bright pages give a better general survey of Africa from the Cape to the Equator than any single volume that has yet been published.'—*Times.*
'A delightful book.'—*Academy.*
'Astonishingly frank. Every page deserves close attention.'—*Literature.*
'Unquestionably one of the most interesting books of travel which have recently appeared.'—*Standard.*
'The honest impressions of a keen-eyed and intrepid traveller.'—*Scotsman.*
'Appealing powerfully to the popular imagination.'—*Globe.*

Henri of Orleans. FROM TONKIN TO INDIA. By PRINCE HENRI OF ORLEANS. Translated by HAMLEY BENT, M.A. With 100 Illustrations and a Map. *Crown 4to, gilt top. 25s.*

'A welcome contribution to our knowledge. The narrative is full and interesting, and the appendices give the work a substantial value.'—*Times.*
'The Prince's travels are of real importance . . . his services to geography have been considerable. The volume is beautifully illustrated.'—*Athenæum.*

R. S. S. Baden-Powell. THE DOWNFALL OF PREMPEH. A Diary of Life in Ashanti, 1895. By Colonel BADEN-POWELL. With 21 Illustrations and a Map. *Cheaper Edition. Large Crown 8vo. 6s.*

'A compact, faithful, most readable record of the campaign.'—*Daily News.*

R. S. S. Baden-Powell. THE MATABELE CAMPAIGN, 1896. By Colonel BADEN-POWELL. With nearly 100 Illustrations. *Cheaper Edition. Large Crown 8vo. 6s.*

'As a straightforward account of a great deal of plucky work unpretentiously done, this book is well worth reading.'—*Times.*

S. L. Hinde. THE FALL OF THE CONGO ARABS. By S. L. HINDE. With Plans, etc. *Demy 8vo. 12s. 6d.*

'The book is full of good things, and of sustained interest.'—*St. James's Gazette.*
'A graphic sketch of one of the most exciting and important episodes in the struggle for supremacy in Central Africa between the Arabs and their European rivals.'—*Times.*

A. St. H. Gibbons. EXPLORATION AND HUNTING IN CENTRAL AFRICA. By Major A. ST. H. GIBBONS, F.R.G.S. With 8 full-page Illustrations by C. WHYMPER, 25 Photographs and Maps. *Demy 8vo.* 15s.

'His book is a grand record of quiet, unassuming, tactful resolution. His adventures were as various as his sporting exploits were exciting.'—*Times.*

E. H. Alderson. WITH THE MOUNTED INFANTRY AND MASHONALAND FIELD FORCE, 1896. By Lieut.-Colonel ALDERSON. With numerous Illustrations and Plans. *Demy 8vo.* 10s. 6d.

'An interesting contribution to the story of the British Empire's growth.'—*Daily News.*

'A clear, vigorous, and soldier-like narrative.'—*Scotsman.*

Seymour Vandeleur. CAMPAIGNING ON THE UPPER NILE AND NIGER. By Lieut. SEYMOUR VANDELEUR. With an Introduction by Sir G. GOLDIE, K.C.M.G. With 4 Maps, Illustrations, and Plans. *Large Crown 8vo.* 10s. 6d.

Upon the African question there is no book procurable which contains so much of value as this one.'—*Guardian.*

Lord Fincastle. A FRONTIER CAMPAIGN. By the Viscount FINCASTLE, V.C., and Lieut. P. C. ELLIOTT-LOCKHART. With a Map and 16 Illustrations. *Second Edition. Crown 8vo.* 6s.

'An admirable book, combining in a volume a piece of pleasant reading for the general reader, and a really valuable treatise on frontier war.'—*Athenæum.*

J. K. Trotter. THE NIGER SOURCES. By Colonel J. K. TROTTER, R.A. With a Map and Illustrations. *Crown 8vo.* 5s.

'A most interesting as well as a lucidly and modestly written book.'—*Spectator.*

Michael Davitt. LIFE AND PROGRESS IN AUSTRALASIA. By MICHAEL DAVITT, M.P. With 2 Maps. *Crown 8vo.* 6s. 500 pp.

'An interesting and suggestive work.'—*Daily Chronicle.*

'Contains an astonishing amount of practical information.'—*Daily Mail.*

'One of the most valuable contributions to our store of Imperial literature that has been published for a very long time.'—*Pall Mall Gazette.*

W. Crooke. THE NORTH-WESTERN PROVINCES OF INDIA: THEIR ETHNOLOGY AND ADMINISTRATION. By W. CROOKE. With Maps and Illustrations. *Demy 8vo.* 10s. 6d.

'A carefully and well-written account of one of the most important provinces of the Empire. Mr. Crooke deals with the land in its physical aspect, the province under Hindoo and Mussulman rule, under British rule, its ethnology and sociology, its religious and social life, the land and its settlement, and the native peasant. The illustrations are good, and the map is excellent.'—*Manchester Guardian.*

A. Boisragon. THE BENIN MASSACRE. By CAPTAIN BOISRAGON. *Second Edition. Crown 8vo.* 3s. 6d.

'If the story had been written four hundred years ago it would be read to-day as an English classic.'—*Scotsman.*

'If anything could enhance the horror and the pathos of this remarkable book it is the simple style of the author, who writes as he would talk, unconscious of his own heroism, with an artlessness which is the highest art.'—*Pall Mall Gazette.*

H. S. Cowper. THE HILL OF THE GRACES: OR, THE GREAT STONE TEMPLES OF TRIPOLI. By H. S. COWPER, F.S.A. With Maps, Plans, and 75 Illustrations. *Demy 8vo.* 10s. 6d.

Forms a valuable chapter of what has now become quite a large and important branch of antiquarian research.'—*Times.*

W. Kinnaird Rose. WITH THE GREEKS IN THESSALY. By W. KINNAIRD ROSE, Reuter's Correspondent. With Plans and 23 Illustrations. *Crown 8vo.* 6s.

W. B. Worsfold. SOUTH AFRICA. By W. B. WORSFOLD, M.A. *With a Map. Second Edition. Crown 8vo.* 6s.

'A monumental work compressed into a very moderate compass.'—*World.*

Naval and Military

G. W. Steevens. NAVAL POLICY: By. G. W. STEEVENS. *Demy 8vo.* 6s.

This book is a description of the British and other more important navies of the world, with a sketch of the lines on which our naval policy might possibly be developed.
'An extremely able and interesting work.'—*Daily Chronicle.*

D. Hannay. A SHORT HISTORY OF THE ROYAL NAVY, FROM EARLY TIMES TO THE PRESENT DAY. By DAVID HANNAY. Illustrated. *2 Vols. Demy 8vo.* 7s. 6d. *each.* Vol. I., 1200-1688.

'We read it from cover to cover at a sitting, and those who go to it for a lively and brisk picture of the past, with all its faults and its grandeur, will not be disappointed. The historian is endowed with literary skill and style.'—*Standard.*
'We can warmly recommend Mr. Hannay's volume to any intelligent student of naval history. Great as is the merit of Mr. Hannay's historical narrative, the merit of his strategic exposition is even greater.'—*Times.*

C. Cooper King. THE STORY OF THE BRITISH ARMY. By Colonel COOPER KING, Illustrated. *Demy 8vo.* 7s. 6d.

An authoritative and accurate story of England's military progress.'—*Daily Mail.*
'This handy volume contains, in a compendious form, a brief but adequate sketch of the story of the British army.'—*Daily News.*

R. Southey. ENGLISH SEAMEN (Howard, Clifford, Hawkins, Drake, Cavendish). By ROBERT SOUTHEY. Edited, with an Introduction, by DAVID HANNAY. *Second Edition. Crown 8vo.* 6s.

'Admirable and well-told stories of our naval history.'—*Army and Navy Gazette.*
'A brave, inspiring book.'—*Black and White.*

W. Clark Russell. THE LIFE OF ADMIRAL LORD COLLINGWOOD. By W. CLARK RUSSELL, With Illustrations by F. BRANGWYN. *Third Edition. Crown 8vo.* 6s.

'A book which we should like to see in the hands of every boy in the country.'—*St. James's Gazette.* 'A really good book.'—*Saturday Review.*

E. L. S. Horsburgh. THE CAMPAIGN OF WATERLOO. By E. L. S. HORSBURGH, B.A. *With Plans. Crown 8vo.* 5s.

'A brilliant essay—simple, sound, and thorough.'—*Daily Chronicle.*

H. B. George. BATTLES OF ENGLISH HISTORY. By H. B. GEORGE, M.A., Fellow of New College, Oxford. With numerous Plans. *Third Edition. Crown 8vo. 6s.*

'Mr. George has undertaken a very useful task—that of making military affairs intelligible and instructive to non-military readers—and has executed it with laudable intelligence and industry, and with a large measure of success.'—*Times.*

General Literature

S. Baring Gould. OLD COUNTRY LIFE. By S. BARING GOULD. With Sixty-seven Illustrations. *Large Crown 8vo. Fifth Edition.* 6s.

'"Old Country Life," as healthy wholesome reading, full of breezy life and movement, full of quaint stories vigorously told, will not be excelled by any book to be published throughout the year. Sound, hearty, and English to the core.'—*World.*

S. Baring Gould. HISTORIC ODDITIES AND STRANGE EVENTS. By S. BARING GOULD. *Fourth Edition. Crown 8vo. 6s.*

'A collection of exciting and entertaining chapters. The whole volume is delightful reading.'—*Times.*

S. Baring Gould. FREAKS OF FANATICISM. By S. BARING GOULD. *Third Edition. Crown 8vo. 6s.*

'A perfectly fascinating book.'—*Scottish Leader.*

S. Baring Gould. A GARLAND OF COUNTRY SONG: English Folk Songs with their Traditional Melodies. Collected and arranged by S. BARING GOULD and H. F. SHEPPARD. *Demy 4to. 6s.*

S. Baring Gould. SONGS OF THE WEST: Traditional Ballads and Songs of the West of England, with their Melodies. Collected by S. BARING GOULD, M.A., and H. F. SHEPPARD, M.A. In 4 Parts. *Parts I., II., III.,* 3s. each. *Part IV.,* 5s. *In one Vol., French morocco,* 15s.

'A rich collection of humour, pathos, grace, and poetic fancy.'—*Saturday Review.*

S. Baring Gould. YORKSHIRE ODDITIES AND STRANGE EVENTS. By S. BARING GOULD. *Fourth Edition. Crown 8vo.* 6s.

S. Baring Gould. STRANGE SURVIVALS AND SUPERSTITIONS. By S. BARING GOULD. *Crown 8vo. Second Edition.* 6s.

S. Baring Gould. THE DESERTS OF SOUTHERN FRANCE. By S. BARING GOULD. 2 *vols. Demy 8vo.* 32s.

Cotton Minchin. OLD HARROW DAYS. By J. G. COTTON MINCHIN. *Crown 8vo. Second Edition.* 5s.

'This book is an admirable record.'—*Daily Chronicle.*

W. E. Gladstone. THE SPEECHES OF THE RT. HON. W. E. GLADSTONE, M.P. Edited by A. W. HUTTON, M.A., and H. J. COHEN, M.A. With Portraits. *Demy 8vo. Vols. IX. and X. 12s. 6d. each.*

E. V. Zenker. ANARCHISM. By E. V. ZENKER. *Demy 8vo. 7s. 6d.*
'Well-written, and full of shrewd comments.'—*The Speaker.*
'Herr Zenker has succeeded in producing a careful and critical history of the growth of Anarchist theory. He is to be congratulated upon a really interesting work.'—*Literature.*

H. G. Hutchinson. THE GOLFING PILGRIM. By HORACE G. HUTCHINSON. *Crown 8vo. 6s.*
'Full of useful information with plenty of good stories.'—*Truth.*
'Without this book the golfer's library will be incomplete.'—*Pall Mall Gazette.*
'We can recommend few books as better company.'—*St. James's Gazette.*
'It will charm all golfers.'—*Times.*
'Decidedly pleasant reading.'—*Athenæum.*

J. Wells. OXFORD AND OXFORD LIFE. By Members of the University. Edited by J. WELLS, M.A., Fellow and Tutor of Wadham College. *Second Edition. Crown 8vo. 3s. 6d.*
'We congratulate Mr. Wells on the production of a readable and intelligent account of Oxford as it is at the present time, written by persons who are possessed of a close acquaintance with the system and life of the University.'—*Athenæum.*

J. Wells. OXFORD AND ITS COLLEGES. By J. WELLS, M.A., Fellow and Tutor of Wadham College. Illustrated by E. H. NEW. *Second Edition. Fcap. 8vo. 3s. Leather. 3s. 6d. net.*
'An admirable and accurate little treatise, attractively illustrated.'—*World.*
'A luminous and tasteful little volume.'—*Daily Chronicle.*
'Exactly what the intelligent visitor wants.'—*Glasgow Herald.*

C. G. Robertson. VOCES ACADEMICÆ. By C. GRANT ROBERTSON, M.A., Fellow of All Souls', Oxford. *With a Frontispiece. Pott. 8vo. 3s. 6d.*
'Decidedly clever and amusing.'—*Athenæum.*
'A clever and entertaining little book.'—*Pall Mall Gazette.*

L. Whibley. GREEK OLIGARCHIES: THEIR ORGANISATION AND CHARACTER. By L. WHIBLEY, M.A., Fellow of Pembroke College, Cambridge. *Crown 8vo. 6s.*
'An exceedingly useful handbook: a careful and well-arranged study.'—*Times.*

L. L. Price. ECONOMIC SCIENCE AND PRACTICE. By L. L. PRICE, M.A., Fellow of Oriel College, Oxford. *Crown 8vo. 6s.*

J. S. Shedlock. THE PIANOFORTE SONATA: Its Origin and Development. By J. S. SHEDLOCK. *Crown 8vo. 5s.*
'This work should be in the possession of every musician and amateur. A concise and lucid history and a very valuable work for reference.'—*Athenæum.*

E. M. Bowden. THE EXAMPLE OF BUDDHA: Being Quotations from Buddhist Literature for each Day in the Year. Compiled by E. M. BOWDEN. *Third Edition. 16mo. 2s. 6d.*

Science and Technology

Freudenreich. DAIRY BACTERIOLOGY. A Short Manual for the Use of Students. By Dr. ED. VON FREUDENREICH. Translated by J. R. AINSWORTH DAVIS, B.A. *Crown 8vo.* 2s. 6d.

Chalmers Mitchell. OUTLINES OF BIOLOGY. By P. CHALMERS MITCHELL, M.A., *Illustrated. Crown 8vo.* 6s.

A text-book designed to cover the new Schedule issued by the Royal College of Physicians and Surgeons.

G. Massee. A MONOGRAPH OF THE MYXOGASTRES. By GEORGE MASSEE. With 12 Coloured Plates. *Royal 8vo.* 18s. *net.*

'A work much in advance of any book in the language treating of this group of organisms. Indispensable to every student of the Myxogastres.'—*Nature.*

Stephenson and Suddards. ORNAMENTAL DESIGN FOR WOVEN FABRICS. By C. STEPHENSON, of The Technical College, Bradford, and F. SUDDARDS, of The Yorkshire College, Leeds. With 65 full-page plates. *Demy 8vo.* 7s. 6d.

'The book is very ably done, displaying an intimate knowledge of principles, good taste, and the faculty of clear exposition.'—*Yorkshire Post.*

TEXT-BOOKS OF TECHNOLOGY.
Edited by PROFESSORS GARNETT and WERTHEIMER.

HOW TO MAKE A DRESS By J. A. E. WOOD. *Illustrated. Crown 8vo.* 1s. 6d.

A text-book for students preparing for the City and Guilds examination, based on the syllabus. The diagrams are numerous.

'Though primarily intended for students, Miss Wood's dainty little manual may be consulted with advantage by any girls who want to make their own frocks. The directions are simple and clear, and the diagrams very helpful.'—*Literature.*

'A splendid little book.'—*Evening News.*

Philosophy

L. T. Hobhouse. THE THEORY OF KNOWLEDGE. By L. T. HOBHOUSE, Fellow of C.C.C, Oxford. *Demy 8vo.* 21s.

'The most important contribution to English philosophy since the publication of Mr. Bradley's "Appearance and Reality."'—*Glasgow Herald.*

'A brilliantly written volume.'—*Times.*

W. H. Fairbrother. THE PHILOSOPHY OF T. H. GREEN. By W. H. FAIRBROTHER, M.A. *Crown 8vo.* 3s. 6d.

'In every way an admirable book.'—*Glasgow Herald.*

F. W. Bussell. THE SCHOOL OF PLATO. By F. W. BUSSELL, D.D., Fellow of Brasenose College, Oxford. *Demy 8vo.* 10s. 6d.

'A highly valuable contribution to the history of ancient thought.'—*Glasgow Herald.*

'A clever and stimulating book,—*Manchester Guardian.*

F. S. Granger. THE WORSHIP OF THE ROMANS. By F. S. GRANGER, M.A., Litt.D., Professor of Philosophy at University College, Nottingham. *Crown 8vo. 6s.*

A scholarly analysis of the religious ceremonies, beliefs, and superstitions of ancient Rome, conducted in the new light of comparative anthropology.'—*Times.*

Theology

Handbooks of Theology.

General Editor, A. ROBERTSON, D.D., Principal of King's College, London.

THE XXXIX. ARTICLES OF THE CHURCH OF ENGLAND. Edited with an Introduction by E. C. S. GIBSON, D.D., Vicar of Leeds, late Principal of Wells Theological College. *Second and Cheaper Edition in One Volume. Demy 8vo. 12s. 6d.*

'Dr. Gibson is a master of clear and orderly exposition. And he has in a high degree a quality very necessary, but rarely found, in commentators on this topic, that of absolute fairness. His book is pre-eminently honest.'—*Times.*
'After a survey of the whole book, we can bear witness to the transparent honesty of purpose, evident industry, and clearness of style which mark its contents. They maintain throughout a very high level of doctrine and tone.'—*Guardian.*
'The most convenient and most acceptable commentary.'—*Expository Times.*

AN INTRODUCTION TO THE HISTORY OF RELIGION. By F. B. JEVONS, M.A., Litt.D., Principal of Bishop Hatfield's Hall. *Demy 8vo. 10s. 6d.*

'Dr. Jevons has written a notable work, which we can strongly recommend to the serious attention of theologians and anthropologists.'—*Manchester Guardian.*
'The merit of this book lies in the penetration, the singular acuteness and force of the author's judgment. He is at once critical and luminous, at once just and suggestive. A comprehensive and thorough book.'—*Birmingham Post.*

THE DOCTRINE OF THE INCARNATION. By R. L. OTTLEY, M.A., late fellow of Magdalen College, Oxon., and Principal of Pusey House. *In Two Volumes. Demy 8vo. 15s.*

'Learned and reverent: lucid and well arranged.'—*Record.*
'A clear and remarkably full account of the main currents of speculation. Scholarly precision . . . genuine tolerance . . . intense interest in his subject—are Mr. Ottley's merits.'—*Guardian.*

The Churchman's Library.

Edited by J. H. BURN, B.D.

THE BEGINNINGS OF ENGLISH CHRISTIANITY. By W. E. COLLINS, M.A., Professor of Ecclesiastical History at King's College, London. With Map. *Crown 8vo. 3s. 6d.*

An investigation in detail, based upon original authorities, of the beginnings of the English Church, with a careful account of earlier Celtic Christianity. Some very full appendices treat of a number of special subjects.
'An excellent example of thorough and fresh historical work.'—*Guardian.*

SOME NEW TESTAMENT PROBLEMS. By ARTHUR WRIGHT, Fellow of Queen's College, Cambridge. *Crown 8vo. 6s.*

'Bold and outspoken; earnest and reverent.'—*Glasgow Herald.*

S R. Driver. SERMONS ON SUBJECTS CONNECTED WITH THE OLD TESTAMENT. By S. R. DRIVER, D.D., Canon of Christ Church, Regius Professor of Hebrew in the University of Oxford. *Crown 8vo.* 6s.

'A welcome companion to the author's famous 'Introduction.'—*Guardian.*

T. K. Cheyne. FOUNDERS OF OLD TESTAMENT CRITICISM. By T. K. CHEYNE, D.D., Oriel Professor at Oxford. *Large crown 8vo.* 7s. 6d.

A historical sketch of O. T. Criticism.
'A very learned and instructive work.'—*Times.*

H. H. Henson. DISCIPLINE AND LAW. By H. HENSLEY HENSON, B.D., Fellow of All Souls', Oxford; Incumbent of St. Mary's Hospital, Ilford; Chaplain to the Bishop of St. Albans. *Fcap. 8vo.* 2s. 6d.

'An admirable little volume of Lent addresses. We warmly commend the general drift of Mr. Henson's book.'—*Guardian.*

H. H. Henson. LIGHT AND LEAVEN: HISTORICAL AND SOCIAL SERMONS. By H. HENSLEY HENSON, M.A. *Crown 8vo.* 6s.

'They are always reasonable as well as vigorous.'—*Scotsman.*

W. H. Bennett. A PRIMER OF THE BIBLE. By Prof. W. H. BENNETT. *Second Edition. Crown 8vo.* 2s. 6d.

'The work of an honest, fearless, and sound critic, and an excellent guide in a small compass to the books of the Bible.'—*Manchester Guardian,*
'A unique primer.'—*English Churchman.*

C. H. Prior. CAMBRIDGE SERMONS. Edited by C. H. PRIOR, M.A., Fellow and Tutor of Pembroke College. *Crown 8vo.* 6s.

A volume of sermons preached before the University of Cambridge by various preachers, including the late Archbishop of Canterbury and Bishop Westcott.

Cecilia Robinson. THE MINISTRY OF DEACONESSES. By Deaconess CECILIA ROBINSON. With an Introduction by the Lord Bishop of Winchester and an Appendix by Professor ARMITAGE ROBINSON. *Crown 8vo.* 3s. 6d.

'A learned and interesting book, combining with no ordinary skill the authority of learned research with the practical utility of a descriptive manual of parish work.'
—*Scotsman.*

E. B. Layard. RELIGION IN BOYHOOD. Notes on the Religious Training of Boys. By E. B. LAYARD, M.A. *18mo.* 1s.

W. Yorke Fausset. THE *DE CATECHIZANDIS RUDIBUS* OF ST. AUGUSTINE. Edited, with Introduction, Notes, etc., by W. YORKE FAUSSET, M.A. *Crown 8vo.* 3s. 6d.

An edition of a Treatise on the Essentials of Christian Doctrine, and the best methods of impressing them on candidates for baptism.

F. Weston. THE HOLY SACRIFICE. By F. WESTON, M.A., Curate of St. Matthew's, Westminster. *Pott 8vo.* 1s.

A small volume of devotions at the Holy Communion, especially adapted to the needs of servers and those who do not communicate.

À Kempis. THE IMITATION OF CHRIST. By THOMAS A KEMPIS. With an Introduction by DEAN FARRAR. Illustrated by C. M. GERE, and printed in black and red. *Second Edition. Fcap. 8vo. Buckram.* 3s. 6d. *Padded morocco,* 5s.

'Amongst all the innumerable English editions of the "Imitation," there can have been few which were prettier than this one, printed in strong and handsome type, with all the glory of red initials.'—*Glasgow Herald.*

J. Keble. THE CHRISTIAN YEAR. By JOHN KEBLE. With an Introduction and Notes by W. LOCK, D.D., Warden of Keble College, Ireland Professor at Oxford. Illustrated by R. ANNING BELL. *Second Edition. Fcap. 8vo. Buckram.* 3s. 6d. *Padded morocco,* 5s.

'The present edition is annotated with all the care and insight to be expected from Mr. Lock. The progress and circumstances of its composition are detailed in the Introduction. There is an interesting Appendix on the MSS. of the "Christian Year," and another giving the order in which the poems were written. A " Short Analysis of the Thought" is prefixed to each, and any difficulty in the text is explained in a note.'—*Guardian.*

The Library of Devotion.

Pott 8vo, cloth. 2s; *leather.* 2s. 6d. *net.*

'This series is excellent.'—THE BISHOP OF LONDON.
'A very delightful edition.'—THE BISHOP OF BATH AND WELLS.
'Well worth the attention of the Clergy.'—THE BISHOP OF LICHFIELD.
'The new "Library of Devotion" is excellent.'—THE BISHOP OF PETERBOROUGH.
'Charming.'—*Record.*
'Delightful.'—*Church Bells.*

THE CONFESSIONS OF ST. AUGUSTINE. Newly Translated, with an Introduction and Notes, by C. BIGG, D.D., late Student of Christ Church. *Second Edition.*

'The translation is an excellent piece of English, and the introduction is a masterly exposition. We augur well of a series which begins so satisfactorily.'—*Times.*
'No translation has appeared in so convenient a form, and none, we think, evidencing so true, so delicate, so feeling a touch.'—*Birmingham Post.*
'Dr. Bigg has made a new and vigorous translation, and has enriched the text with a luminous introduction and pithy notes.'—*Speaker.*

THE CHRISTIAN YEAR. By JOHN KEBLE. With Introduction and Notes by WALTER LOCK, D.D., Warden of Keble College, Ireland Professor at Oxford.

'No prettier book could be desired.'—*Manchester Guardian.*
'The volume is very prettily bound and printed, and may fairly claim to be an advance on any previous editions.'—*Guardian.*
'The introduction is admirable, and admirers of Keble will be greatly interested in the chronological list of the poems.'—*Bookman.*

THE IMITATION OF CHRIST. A Revised Translation, with an Introduction, by C. BIGG, D.D., late Student of Christ Church.

Dr. Bigg has made a practically new translation of this book, which the reader will have, almost for the first time, exactly in the shape in which it left the hands of the author.
'The text is at once scholarly in its faithful reproduction in English of the sonorous Church Latin in which the original is composed, and popular in the sense of being simple and intelligible.'—*Scotsman.*

Leaders of Religion

Edited by H. C. BEECHING, M.A. *With Portraits, crown 8vo. 3s. 6d.*

A series of short biographies of the most prominent leaders of religious life and thought of all ages and countries.

The following are ready—

CARDINAL NEWMAN. By R. H. HUTTON.
JOHN WESLEY. By J. H. OVERTON, M.A.
BISHOP WILBERFORCE. By G. W. DANIELL, M.A.
CARDINAL MANNING. By A. W. HUTTON, M.A.
CHARLES SIMEON. By H. C. G. MOULE, D.D.
JOHN KEBLE. By WALTER LOCK, D.D.
THOMAS CHALMERS. By Mrs. OLIPHANT.
LANCELOT ANDREWES. By R. L. OTTLEY, M.A.
AUGUSTINE OF CANTERBURY. By E. L. CUTTS, D.D.
WILLIAM LAUD. By W. H. HUTTON, B.D.
JOHN KNOX. By F. MACCUNN.
JOHN HOWE. By R. F. HORTON, D.D.
BISHOP KEN. By F. A. CLARKE, M.A.
GEORGE FOX, THE QUAKER. By T. HODGKIN, D.C.L.
JOHN DONNE. By AUGUSTUS JESSOPP, D.D.
THOMAS CRANMER. By A. J. MASON.

Other volumes will be announced in due course.

Fiction

SIX SHILLING NOVELS
Marie Corelli's Novels
Crown 8vo. 6s. each.

A ROMANCE OF TWO WORLDS. *Eighteenth Edition.*
VENDETTA. *Fourteenth Edition.*
THELMA. *Twentieth Edition.*
ARDATH. *Eleventh Edition.*
THE SOUL OF LILITH *Ninth Edition.*
WORMWOOD. *Ninth Edition.*
BARABBAS: A DREAM OF THE WORLD'S TRAGEDY. *Thirty-third Edition.*

'The tender reverence of the treatment and the imaginative beauty of the writing have reconciled us to the daring of the conception, and the conviction is forced on us that even so exalted a subject cannot be made too familiar to us, provided it be presented in the true spirit of Christian faith. The amplifications of the Scripture narrative are often conceived with high poetic insight, and this "Dream of the World's Tragedy" is a lofty and not inadequate paraphrase of the supreme climax of the inspired narrative.'—*Dublin Review.*

THE SORROWS OF SATAN. *Thirty-ninth Edition.*

'A very powerful piece of work. . . . The conception is magnificent, and is likely to win an abiding place within the memory of man. . . . The author has immense command of language, and a limitless audacity. . . . This interesting and remarkable romance will live long after much of the ephemeral literature of the day is forgotten. . . . A literary phenomenon . . . novel, and even sublime.'—W. T. STEAD in the *Review of Reviews.*

Anthony Hope's Novels
Crown 8vo. 6s. each.

THE GOD IN THE CAR. *Eighth Edition.*
'A very remarkable book, deserving of critical analysis impossible within our limit; brilliant, but not superficial; well considered, but not elaborated; constructed with the proverbial art that conceals, but yet allows itself to be enjoyed by readers to whom fine literary method is a keen pleasure.'—*The World.*

A CHANGE OF AIR. *Fifth Edition.*
'A graceful, vivacious comedy, true to human nature. The characters are traced with a masterly hand.'—*Times.*

A MAN OF MARK. *Fourth Edition.*
'Of all Mr. Hope's books, "A Man of Mark" is the one which best compares with "The Prisoner of Zenda."'—*National Observer.*

THE CHRONICLES OF COUNT ANTONIO. *Third Edition.*
'It is a perfectly enchanting story of love and chivalry, and pure romance. The Count is the most constant, desperate, and modest and tender of lovers, a peerless gentleman, an intrepid fighter, a faithful friend, and a magnanimous foe.'—*Guardian.*

PHROSO. Illustrated by H. R. MILLAR. *Third Edition.*
'The tale is thoroughly fresh, quick with vitality, stirring the blood, and humorously, dashingly told.'—*St. James's Gazette.*
'A story of adventure, every page of which is palpitating with action.'—*Speaker.*
'From cover to cover "Phroso" not only engages the attention, but carries the reader in little whirls of delight from adventure to adventure.'—*Academy.*

SIMON DALE. By ANTHONY HOPE. Illustrated. *Third Edition. Crown 8vo. 6s.*
'"Simon Dale" is one of the best historical romances that have been written for a long while.'—*St. James's Gazette.*
'A bright and gallant story.'—*Graphic.*
'A brilliant novel. The story is rapid and most excellently told. As for the hero, he is a perfect hero of romance—he is brave, witty, adventurous, and a good lover.'—*Athenæum.*
'There is searching analysis of human nature, with a most ingeniously constructed plot. Mr. Hope has drawn the contrasts of his women with marvellous subtlety and delicacy. This love-story of 200 years ago makes the man and the woman live again.'—*Times.*

S. Baring Gould's Novels
Crown 8vo. 6s. each.

'To say that a book is by the author of "Mehalah" is to imply that it contains a story cast on strong lines, containing dramatic possibilities, vivid and sympathetic descriptions of Nature, and a wealth of ingenious imagery.'—*Speaker.*
'That whatever Mr. Baring Gould writes is well worth reading, is a conclusion that may be very generally accepted. His views of life are fresh and vigorous, his language pointed and characteristic, the incidents of which he makes use are striking and original, his characters are life-like, and though somewhat exceptional people, are drawn and coloured with artistic force. Add to this that his descriptions of scenes and scenery are painted with the loving eyes and skilled hands of a master of his art, that he is always fresh and never dull, and it is no wonder that readers have gained confidence in his power of amusing and satisfying them, and that year by year his popularity widens.'—*Court Circular.*

ARMINELL. *Fourth Edition.*
URITH. *Fifth Edition.*
IN THE ROAR OF THE SEA. *Sixth Edition.*
MRS. CURGENVEN OF CURGENVEN. *Fourth Edition.*

CHEAP JACK ZITA. *Fourth Edition.*
THE QUEEN OF LOVE. *Fourth Edition.*
MARGERY OF QUETHER. *Third Edition.*
JACQUETTA. *Third Edition.*
KITTY ALONE. *Fifth Edition.*
NOÉMI. Illustrated by R. C. WOODVILLE. *Third Edition.*
THE BROOM-SQUIRE. Illustrated by F DADD. *Fourth Edition.*
THE PENNYCOMEQUICKS. *Third Edition.*
DARTMOOR IDYLLS.
GUAVAS THE TINNER. Illustrated by F. DADD. *Second Edition.*
BLADYS. Illustrated. *Second Edition.*

Gilbert Parker's Novels
Crown 8vo. 6s. each.

PIERRE AND HIS PEOPLE. *Fourth Edition.*
'Stories happily conceived and finely executed. There is strength and genius in Mr. Parker's style.'—*Daily Telegraph.*

MRS. FALCHION. *Fourth Edition.*
'A splendid study of character.'—*Athenæum.*
'But little behind anything that has been done by any writer of our time.'—*Pall Mall Gazette.*   'A very striking and admirable novel.'—*St. James's Gazette.*

THE TRANSLATION OF A SAVAGE.
'The plot is original and one difficult to work out; but Mr. Parker has done it with great skill and delicacy. The reader who is not interested in this original, fresh, and well-told tale must be a dull person indeed.'—*Daily Chronicle.*

THE TRAIL OF THE SWORD. *Illustrated. Sixth Edition.*
'A rousing and dramatic tale. A book like this, in which swords flash, great surprises are undertaken, and daring deeds done, in which men and women live and love in the old passionate way, is a joy inexpressible.'—*Daily Chronicle.*

WHEN VALMOND CAME TO PONTIAC: The Story of a Lost Napoleon. *Fourth Edition.*
'Here we find romance—real, breathing, living romance. The character of Valmond is drawn unerringly. The book must be read, we may say re-read, for any one thoroughly to appreciate Mr. Parker's delicate touch and innate sympathy with humanity.'—*Pall Mall Gazette.*

AN ADVENTURER OF THE NORTH: The Last Adventures of 'Pretty Pierre.' *Second Edition.*
'The present book is full of fine and moving stories of the great North, and it will add to Mr. Parker's already high reputation.'—*Glasgow Herald.*

THE SEATS OF THE MIGHTY. *Illustrated. Ninth Edition.*
'The best thing he has done; one of the best things that any one has done lately.'—*St. James's Gazette.*
'Mr. Parker seems to become stronger and easier with every serious novel that he attempts. He shows the matured power which his former novels have led us to expect, and has produced a really fine historical novel.'—*Athenæum.*
'A great book.'—*Black and White.*
'One of the strongest stories of historical interest and adventure that we have read for many a day. . . . A notable and successful book.'—*Speaker.*

THE POMP OF THE LAVILETTES. *Second Edition.* 3s. 6d.
'Living, breathing romance, genuine and unforced pathos, and a deeper and more subtle knowledge of human nature than Mr. Parker has ever displayed before. It is, in a word, the work of a true artist.'—*Pall Mall Gazette.*

Conan Doyle. ROUND THE RED LAMP. By A. CONAN DOYLE. *Sixth Edition. Crown 8vo. 6s.*
'The book is far and away the best view that has been vouchsafed us behind the scenes of the consulting-room.'—*Illustrated London News.*

Stanley Weyman. UNDER THE RED ROBE. By STANLEY WEYMAN, Author of 'A Gentleman of France.' With Illustrations by R. C. Woodville. *Fourteenth Edition. Crown 8vo. 6s.*
'A book of which we have read every word for the sheer pleasure of reading, and which we put down with a pang that we cannot forget it all and start again.'—*Westminster Gazette.*
'Every one who reads books at all must read this thrilling romance, from the first page of which to the last the breathless reader is haled along. An inspiration of manliness and courage.'—*Daily Chronicle.*

Lucas Malet. THE WAGES OF SIN. By LUCAS MALET. *Thirteenth Edition. Crown 8vo. 6s.*

Lucas Malet. THE CARISSIMA. By LUCAS MALET, Author of 'The Wages of Sin,' etc. *Third Edition. Crown 8vo. 6s.*

S. R. Crockett. LOCHINVAR. By S. R. CROCKETT, Author of 'The Raiders,' etc. Illustrated. *Second Edition. Crown 8vo. 6s.*
'Full of gallantry and pathos, of the clash of arms, and brightened by episodes of humour and love. . . . Mr. Crockett has never written a stronger or better book.' —*Westminster Gazette.*

S. R. Crockett. THE STANDARD BEARER. By S. R. CROCKETT. *Crown 8vo. 6s.*
'A delightful tale in his best style.'—*Speaker.*
'Mr. Crockett at his best.'—*Literature.*
'Enjoyable and of absorbing interest.'—*Scotsman.*

Arthur Morrison. TALES OF MEAN STREETS. By ARTHUR MORRISON. *Fifth Edition. Crown 8vo. 6s.*
'Told with consummate art and extraordinary detail. In the true humanity of the book lies its justification, the permanence of its interest, and its indubitable triumph.'—*Athenæum.*
'A great book. The author's method is amazingly effective, and produces a thrilling sense of reality. The writer lays upon us a master hand. The book is simply appalling and irresistible in its interest. It is humorous also; without humour it would not make the mark it is certain to make.'—*World.*

Arthur Morrison. A CHILD OF THE JAGO. By ARTHUR MORRISON. *Third Edition. Crown 8vo. 6s.*
'The book is a masterpiece.'—*Pall Mall Gazette.*
'Told with great vigour and powerful simplicity.'—*Athenæum.*

Mrs. Clifford. A FLASH OF SUMMER. By Mrs. W. K. CLIFFORD, Author of 'Aunt Anne,' etc. *Second Edition. Crown 8vo. 6s.*

'The story is a very beautiful one, exquisitely told.'—*Speaker.*

Emily Lawless. HURRISH. By the Honble. EMILY LAWLESS, Author of 'Maelcho,' etc. *Fifth Edition. Crown 8vo. 6s.*

Emily Lawless. MAELCHO: a Sixteenth Century Romance. By the Honble. EMILY LAWLESS. *Second Edition. Crown 8vo. 6s.*

'A really great book.'—*Spectator.*
'There is no keener pleasure in life than the recognition of genius. A piece of work of the first order, which we do not hesitate to describe as one of the most remarkable literary achievements of this generation.'—*Manchester Guardian.*

Emily Lawless. TRAITS AND CONFIDENCES. By The Honble. EMILY LAWLESS. *Crown 8vo. 6s.*

'A very charming little volume. A book which cannot be read without pleasure and profit, written in excellent English, full of delicate spirit, and a keen appreciation of nature, human and inanimate.'—*Pall Mall Gazette.*

Jane Barlow. A CREEL OF IRISH STORIES. By JANE BARLOW, Author of 'Irish Idylls.' *Second Edition. Crown 8vo. 6s.*

'Vivid and singularly real.'—*Scotsman.*

J. H. Findlater. THE GREEN GRAVES OF BALGOWRIE. By JANE H. FINDLATER. *Fourth Edition. Crown 8vo. 6s.*

'A powerful and vivid story.'—*Standard.*
'A beautiful story, sad and strange as truth itself.'—*Vanity Fair.*
'A very charming and pathetic tale.'—*Pall Mall Gazette.*
'A singularly original, clever, and beautiful story.'—*Guardian.*
'Reveals to us a new writer of undoubted faculty and reserve force.'—*Spectator.*
'An exquisite idyll, delicate, affecting, and beautiful.'—*Black and White.*

J. H. Findlater. A DAUGHTER OF STRIFE. By JANE HELEN FINDLATER. *Crown 8vo. 6s.*

'A story of strong human interest.'—*Scotsman.*
'Her thought has solidity and maturity.'—*Daily Mail.*

Mary Findlater. OVER THE HILLS. By MARY FINDLATER. *Second Edition. Crown 8vo. 6s.*

'A strong and fascinating piece of work.'—*Scotsman.*
'A charming romance, and full of incident. The book is fresh and strong.'—*Speaker.*
'Will make the author's name loved in many a household.'—*Literary World.*
'A strong and wise book of deep insight and unflinching truth.'—*Birmingham Post.*

H. G. Wells. THE STOLEN BACILLUS, and other Stories. By H. G. WELLS. *Second Edition. Crown 8vo. 6s.*

'They are the impressions of a very striking imagination, which, it would seem, has a great deal within its reach.'—*Saturday Review.*

H. G. Wells. THE PLATTNER STORY AND OTHERS. By H. G. WELLS. *Second Edition. Crown 8vo.* 6s.

'Weird and mysterious, they seem to hold the reader as by a magic spell.'—*Scotsman.*
'No volume has appeared for a long time so likely to give equal pleasure to the simplest reader and to the most fastidious critic.'—*Academy.*

Sara Jeanette Duncan. A VOYAGE OF CONSOLATION. By SARA JEANETTE DUNCAN, Author of 'An American Girl in London.' Illustrated. *Third Edition. Crown 8vo.* 6s.

'Humour, pure and spontaneous and irresistible.'—*Daily Mail.*
'A most delightfully bright book.'—*Daily Telegraph.*
'Eminently amusing and entertaining.'—*Outlook.*
'The dialogue is full of wit.'—*Globe.*
'Laughter lurks in every page.'—*Daily News.*

E. F. Benson. DODO: A DETAIL OF THE DAY. By E. F. BENSON. *Sixteenth Edition. Crown 8vo.* 6s.

'A delightfully witty sketch of society.'—*Spectator.*
'A perpetual feast of epigram and paradox.'—*Speaker.*

E. F. Benson. THE RUBICON. By E. F. BENSON, Author of 'Dodo.' *Fifth Edition. Crown 8vo.* 6s.

E. F. Benson. THE VINTAGE. By E. F. BENSON. Author of 'Dodo.' Illustrated by G. P. JACOMB-HOOD. Third Edition. *Crown 8vo.* 6s.

'An excellent piece of romantic literature; a very graceful and moving story. We are struck with the close observation of life in Greece.'—*Saturday Review.*
'Full of fire, earnestness, and beauty.'—*The World.*
'An original and vigorous historical romance.'—*Morning Post.*

Mrs. Oliphant. SIR ROBERT'S FORTUNE. By Mrs. OLIPHANT. *Crown 8vo.* 6s.

'Full of her own peculiar charm of style and character-painting.'—*Pall Mall Gazette.*

Mrs. Oliphant. THE TWO MARYS. By Mrs. OLIPHANT. *Second Edition. Crown 8vo.* 6s.

Mrs. Oliphant. THE LADY'S WALK. By Mrs. OLIPHANT. *Second Edition. Crown 8vo.* 6s.

'A story of exquisite tenderness, of most delicate fancy.'—*Pall Mall Gazette.*

W. E. Norris. MATTHEW AUSTIN. By W. E. NORRIS, Author of 'Mademoiselle de Mersac,' etc. *Fourth Edition. Crown 8vo.* 6s.

'An intellectually satisfactory and morally bracing novel.'—*Daily Telegraph.*

W. E. Norris. HIS GRACE. By W. E. NORRIS. *Third Edition. Crown 8vo.* 6s.

'Mr. Norris has drawn a really fine character in the Duke of Hurstbourne.—*Athenæum.*

W. E. Norris. THE DESPOTIC LADY AND OTHERS. By W. E. NORRIS. *Crown 8vo.* 6s.

'A budget of good fiction of which no one will tire.'—*Scotsman.*

W. E. Norris. CLARISSA FURIOSA. By W. E. NORRIS, *Crown 8vo. 6s.*

'As a story it is admirable, as a *jeu d'esprit* it is capital, as a lay sermon studded with gems of wit and wisdom it is a model.'—*The World.*

W. Clark Russell. MY DANISH SWEETHEART. By W. CLARK RUSSELL. *Illustrated. Fourth Edition. Crown 8vo. 6s.*

Robert Barr. IN THE MIDST OF ALARMS. By ROBERT BARR. *Third Edition. Crown 8vo. 6s.*

'A book which has abundantly satisfied us by its capital humour.'—*Daily Chronicle.*
'Mr. Barr has achieved a triumph.'—*Pall Mall Gazette.*

Robert Barr. THE MUTABLE MANY. By ROBERT BARR, Author of 'In the Midst of Alarms,' 'A Woman Intervenes,' etc. *Second Edition. Crown 8vo. 6s.*

'Very much the best novel that Mr. Barr has yet given us. There is much insight in it, and much excellent humour.'—*Daily Chronicle.*
'An excellent story. It contains several excellently studied characters.'—*Glasgow Herald.*

J. Maclaren Cobban. THE KING OF ANDAMAN: A Saviour of Society. By J. MACLAREN COBBAN. *Crown 8vo. 6s.*

'An unquestionably interesting book. It contains one character, at least, who has in him the root of immortality.'—*Pall Mall Gazette.*

J. Maclaren Cobban. WILT THOU HAVE THIS WOMAN? By J. M. COBBAN, Author of 'The King of Andaman.' *Crown 8vo. 6s.*

M. E. Francis. MISS ERIN. By M. E. FRANCIS, Author of 'In a Northern Village.' *Second Edition. Crown 8vo. 6s.*

'A clever and charming story.'—*Scotsman.*
'Perfectly delightful.'—*Daily Mail.*
'An excellently fancied love tale.'—*Athenæum.*

Robert Hichens. BYEWAYS. By ROBERT HICHENS. Author of 'Flames,' etc. *Second Edition. Crown 8vo. 6s.*

'A very high artistic instinct and striking command of language raise Mr. Hichens' work far above the ruck.'—*Pall Mall Gazette.*
'The work is undeniably that of a man of striking imagination.'—*Daily News.*

Percy White. A PASSIONATE PILGRIM. By PERCY WHITE, Author of 'Mr. Bailey-Martin.' *Crown 8vo. 6s.*

'A work which it is not hyperbole to describe as of rare excellence.'—*Pall Mall Gazette.*
'The clever book of a shrewd and clever author.'—*Athenæum.*

W. Pett Ridge. SECRETARY TO BAYNE, M.P. By W. PETT RIDGE. *Crown 8vo. 6s.*

'Sparkling, vivacious, adventurous.—*St. James's Gazette.*
'Ingenious, amusing, and especially smart.'—*World.*

J. S. Fletcher. THE BUILDERS. By J. S. FLETCHER, Author of 'When Charles I. was King.' *Second Edition. Crown 8vo. 6s.*

'Replete with delightful descriptions.'—*Vanity Fair.*
'The background of country life has never been sketched more realistically.'—*World.*

Andrew Balfour. BY STROKE OF SWORD. By ANDREW BALFOUR. Illustrated by W. CUBITT COOKE. *Fourth Edition. Crown 8vo. 6s.*

'A banquet of good things.'—*Academy.*
'A recital of thrilling interest, told with unflagging vigour.'—*Globe.*
'An unusually excellent example of a semi-historic romance.'—*World.*
'Manly, healthy, and patriotic.'—*Glasgow Herald.*

J. B. Burton. IN THE DAY OF ADVERSITY. By J. BLOUNDELLE-BURTON.' *Second Edition. Crown 8vo. 6s.*

'Unusually interesting and full of highly dramatic situations.—*Guardian.*

J. B. Burton. DENOUNCED. By J. BLOUNDELLE-BURTON. *Second Edition. Crown 8vo 6s.*

J. B. Burton. THE CLASH OF ARMS. By J. BLOUNDELLE-BURTON. *Second Edition. Crown 8vo. 6s.*

'A brave story—brave in deed, brave in word, brave in thought.'—*St. James's Gazette.*
'A fine, manly, spirited piece of work.'—*World.*

J. B. Burton. ACROSS THE SALT SEAS. By J. BLOUNDELLE-BURTON. *Crown 8vo. 6s.*

'The very essence of the true romantic spirit.'—*Truth.*
'An ingenious and exciting story.'—*Manchester Guardian.*
'Singularly well written.'—*Athenæum.*

W. C. Scully. THE WHITE HECATOMB. By W. C. SCULLY, Author of 'Kafir Stories.' *Crown 8vo. 6s.*

'Reveals a marvellously intimate understanding of the Kaffir mind.'—*African Critic.*

W. C. Scully. BETWEEN SUN AND SAND. By W. C. SCULLY, Author of 'The White Hecatomb.' *Crown 8vo. 6s.*

'The reader will find the interest of absolute novelty.'—*The Graphic.*
'The reader passes at once into the very atmosphere of the African desert: the inexpressible space and stillness swallow him up, and there is no world for him but that immeasurable waste.'—*Athenæum.*
'Strong, simple, direct.'—*Daily Chronicle.*
'One of the most enthralling tales we have read.'—*World.*

Victor Waite. CROSS TRAILS. By VICTOR WAITE. Illustrated. *Crown 8vo. 6s.*

'Every page is enthralling.'—*Academy.*
'Full of strength and reality.'—*Athenæum.*
'The book is exceedingly powerful.'—*Glasgow Herald.*

I. Hooper. THE SINGER OF MARLY. By I. HOOPER. Illustrated by W. CUBITT COOKE. *Crown 8vo. 6s.*

'The characters are all picturesque.'—*Scotsman.*
'A novel as vigorous as it is charming.'—*Literary World.*

M. C. Balfour. THE FALL OF THE SPARROW. By M. C. BALFOUR. *Crown 8vo. 6s.*

'It is unusually powerful, and the characterization is uncommonly good.'—*World.*

H. Morrah. A SERIOUS COMEDY. By HERBERT MORRAH. *Crown 8vo. 6s.*

H. Morrah. THE FAITHFUL CITY. By HERBERT MORRAH, Author of 'A Serious Comedy.' *Crown 8vo.* 6s.

L. B. Walford. SUCCESSORS TO THE TITLE. By Mrs. WALFORD, Author of 'Mr. Smith,' etc. *Second Edition. Crown 8vo.* 6s.

Mary Gaunt. KIRKHAM'S FIND. By MARY GAUNT, Author of 'The Moving Finger.' *Crown 8vo.* 6s.

'A really charming novel.'—*Standard.*

M. M. Dowie. GALLIA. By MÉNIE MURIEL DOWIE, Author of 'A Girl in the Karpathians.' *Third Edition. Crown 8vo.* 6s.

'The style is generally admirable, the dialogue not seldom brilliant, the situations surprising in their freshness and originality.'—*Saturday Review.*

M. M. Dowie. THE CROOK OF THE BOUGH. By MENIE MURIEL DOWIE. *Crown 8vo.* 6s.

'An exceptionally clever and well-written book.'—*Daily Telegraph.*
'An excellent story with shrewd humour and bright writing. The author is delightfully witty.'—*Pall Mall Gazette.*
'Strong, suggestive, and witty.'—*Daily News.*

J. A. Barry. IN THE GREAT DEEP. By J. A. BARRY. Author of 'Steve Brown's Bunyip.' *Crown 8vo.* 6s.

'A collection of really admirable short stories of the sea.'—*Westminster Gazette.*

Julian Corbett. A BUSINESS IN GREAT WATERS. By JULIAN CORBETT. *Second Edition. Crown 8vo.* 6s.

J. B. Patton. BIJLI, THE DANCER. By JAMES BLYTHE PATTON. Illustrated. *Crown 8vo.* 6s.

'Powerful and fascinating.'—*Pall Mall Gazette.*
'A true and entrancing book.'—*Country Life Illustrated.*
'A remarkable book.'—*Bookman.*
'A vivid picture of Indian life.'—*Academy.*

Norma Lorimer. JOSIAH'S WIFE. By NORMA LORIMER. *Second Edition. Crown 8vo.* 6s.

'Written in a bright and witty style.'—*Pall Mall Gazette.*

Lucy Maynard. THE PHILANTHROPIST. By LUCY MAYNARD. *Crown 8vo.* 6s.

'It contains many graphic sketches of the private life of a charitable institution.'—*Glasgow Herald.*

L. Cope Cornford. CAPTAIN JACOBUS: A ROMANCE OF THE ROAD. By L. COPE CORNFORD. Illustrated. *Crown 8vo.* 6s.

'An exceptionally good story of adventure and character.'—*World.*

L. Cope Cornford. SONS OF ADVERSITY. By L. COPE CORNFORD, Author of 'Captain Jacobus.' *Crown 8vo.* 6s.

'A very stirring and spirited sketch of the spacious times of Queen Elizabeth.'—*Pall Mall Gazette.*
'Packed with incident.'—*Outlook.*

F. Brune. VAUSSORE. By FRANCIS BRUNE. *Crown 8vo.* 6s.

'A subtle, complete achievement.'—*Pall Mall Gazette.*
'This story is strangely interesting.'—*Manchester Guardian.*

OTHER SIX-SHILLING NOVELS
Crown 8vo.

THE KING OF ALBERIA. By LAURA DAINTREY.
THE DAUGHTER OF ALOUETTE. By MARY A. OWEN.
CHILDREN OF THIS WORLD. By ELLEN F. PINSENT.
AN ELECTRIC SPARK. By G. MANVILLE FENN.
UNDER SHADOW OF THE MISSION. By L. S. McCHESNEY.
THE SPECULATORS. By J. F. BREWER.
THE SPIRIT OF STORM. By RONALD ROSS.
THE QUEENSBERRY CUP. By CLIVE P. WOLLEY.
A HOME IN INVERESK. By T. L. PATON.
MISS ARMSTRONG'S AND OTHER CIRCUMSTANCES. By JOHN DAVIDSON.
DR. CONGALTON'S LEGACY. By HENRY JOHNSTON.
TIME AND THE WOMAN. By RICHARD PRYCE.
THIS MAN'S DOMINION. By the Author of 'A High Little World.'
DIOGENES OF LONDON. By H. B. MARRIOTT WATSON.
THE STONE DRAGON. By MURRAY GILCHRIST.
A VICAR'S WIFE. By EVELYN DICKINSON.
ELSA. By E. M'QUEEN GRAY.

THREE-AND-SIXPENNY NOVELS
Crown 8vo.

DERRICK VAUGHAN, NOVELIST. By EDNA LYALL.
THE KLOOF BRIDE. By ERNEST GLANVILLE.
SUBJECT TO VANITY. By MARGARET BENSON.
THE SIGN OF THE SPIDER. By BERTRAM MITFORD.
THE MOVING FINGER. By MARY GAUNT.
JACO TRELOAR. By J. H. PEARCE.
THE DANCE OF THE HOURS. By 'VERA.'
A WOMAN OF FORTY. By ESMÉ STUART.
A CUMBERER OF THE GROUND. By CONSTANCE SMITH.
THE SIN OF ANGELS. By EVELYN DICKINSON.
AUT DIABOLUS AUT NIHIL. By X. L.
THE COMING OF CUCULAIN. By STANDISH O'GRADY.
THE GODS GIVE MY DONKEY WINGS. By ANGUS EVAN ABBOTT.
THE STAR GAZERS. By G. MANVILLE FENN.
THE POISON OF ASPS. By R. ORTON PROWSE.
THE QUIET MRS. FLEMING. By R. PRYCE.
DISENCHANTMENT. By F. MABEL ROBINSON.

THE SQUIRE OF WANDALES. By A. SHIELD.
A REVEREND GENTLEMAN. By J. M. COBBAN.
A DEPLORABLE AFFAIR. By W. E. NORRIS.
A CAVALIER'S LADYE. By Mrs. DICKER.
THE PRODIGALS. By Mrs. OLIPHANT.
THE SUPPLANTER. By P. NEUMANN.
A MAN WITH BLACK EYELASHES. By H. A. KENNEDY.
A HANDFUL OF EXOTICS. By S. GORDON.
AN ODD EXPERIMENT. By HANNAH LYNCH.
SCOTTISH BORDER LIFE. By JAMES C. DIBDIN.

HALF-CROWN NOVELS
Crown 8vo.

HOVENDEN, V.C. By F. MABEL ROBINSON.
THE PLAN OF CAMPAIGN. By F. MABEL ROBINSON.
MR. BUTLER'S WARD. By F. MABEL ROBINSON.
ELI'S CHILDREN. By G. MANVILLE FENN.
A DOUBLE KNOT. By G. MANVILLE FENN.
DISARMED. By M. BETHAM EDWARDS.
A MARRIAGE AT SEA. By W. CLARK RUSSELL.
IN TENT AND BUNGALOW. By the Author of 'Indian Idylls.'
MY STEWARDSHIP. By E. M'QUEEN GRAY.
JACK'S FATHER. By W. E. NORRIS.
A LOST ILLUSION. By LESLIE KEITH.

THE TRUE HISTORY OF JOSHUA DAVIDSON, Christian and Communist. By E. LYNN LYNTON. *Eleventh Edition. Post 8vo.* 1s.

Books for Boys and Girls
A Series of Books by well-known Authors, well illustrated.

THREE-AND-SIXPENCE EACH

THE ICELANDER'S SWORD. By S. BARING GOULD.
TWO LITTLE CHILDREN AND CHING. By EDITH E. CUTHELL.
TODDLEBEN'S HERO. By M. M. BLAKE.
ONLY A GUARD-ROOM DOG. By EDITH E. CUTHELL.
THE DOCTOR OF THE JULIET. By HARRY COLLINGWOOD.
MASTER ROCKAFELLAR'S VOYAGE. By W. CLARK RUSSELL.
SYD BELTON: Or, The Boy who would not go to Sea. By G. MANVILLE FENN.
THE WALLYPUG IN LONDON. By G. E. FARROW.

The Peacock Library
A Series of Books for Girls by well-known Authors, handsomely bound, and well illustrated.

THREE-AND-SIXPENCE EACH

A PINCH OF EXPERIENCE. By L. B. WALFORD.
THE RED GRANGE. By Mrs. MOLESWORTH.
THE SECRET OF MADAME DE MONLUC. By the Author of 'Mdle Mori.

DUMPS. By Mrs. PARR.
OUT OF THE FASHION. By L. T. MEADE.
A GIRL OF THE PEOPLE. By L. T. MEADE.
HEPSY GIPSY. By L. T. MEADE. 2s. 6d.
THE HONOURABLE MISS. By L. T. MEADE.
MY LAND OF BEULAH. By Mrs. LEITH ADAMS.

University Extension Series

A series of books on historical, literary, and scientific subjects, suitable for extension students and home-reading circles. Each volume is complete in itself, and the subjects are treated by competent writers in a broad and philosophic spirit.

Edited by J. E. SYMES, M.A.,
Principal of University College, Nottingham.
Crown 8vo. Price (with some exceptions) 2s. 6d.
The following volumes are ready:—

THE INDUSTRIAL HISTORY OF ENGLAND. By H. DE B. GIBBINS, D.Litt., M.A., late Scholar of Wadham College, Oxon., Cobden Prizeman. *Sixth Edition, Revised. With Maps and Plans.* 3s.
   'A compact and clear story of our industrial development. A study of this concise but luminous book cannot fail to give the reader a clear insight into the principal phenomena of our industrial history. The editor and publishers are to be congratulated on this first volume of their venture, and we shall look with expectant interest for the succeeding volumes of the series.'—*University Extension Journal.*
A HISTORY OF ENGLISH POLITICAL ECONOMY. By L. L. PRICE, M.A., Fellow of Oriel College, Oxon. *Second Edition.*
PROBLEMS OF POVERTY: An Inquiry into the Industrial Conditions of the Poor. By J. A. HOBSON, M.A. *Third Edition.*
VICTORIAN POETS. By A. SHARP.
THE FRENCH REVOLUTION. By J. E. SYMES, M.A.
PSYCHOLOGY. By F. S. GRANGER, M.A. *Second Edition.*
THE EVOLUTION OF PLANT LIFE: Lower Forms. By G. MASSEE. *With Illustrations.*
AIR AND WATER. By V. B. LEWES, M.A. *Illustrated.*
THE CHEMISTRY OF LIFE AND HEALTH. By C. W. KIMMINS, M.A. *Illustrated.*
THE MECHANICS OF DAILY LIFE. By V. P. SELLS, M.A. *Illustrated.*
ENGLISH SOCIAL REFORMERS. By H. DE B. GIBBINS, D.Litt., M.A.
ENGLISH TRADE AND FINANCE IN THE SEVENTEENTH CENTURY. By W. A. S. HEWINS, B.A.
THE CHEMISTRY OF FIRE. The Elementary Principles of Chemistry. By M. M. PATTISON MUIR, M.A. *Illustrated.*
A TEXT-BOOK OF AGRICULTURAL BOTANY. By M. C. POTTER, M.A., F.L.S. *Illustrated.* 3s. 6d.
THE VAULT OF HEAVEN. A Popular Introduction to Astronomy. By R. A. GREGORY. *With numerous Illustrations.*
METEOROLOGY. The Elements of Weather and Climate. By H. N. DICKSON, F.R.S.E., F.R. Met. Soc. *Illustrated.*
A MANUAL OF ELECTRICAL SCIENCE. By GEORGE J. BURCH, M.A. *With numerous Illustrations.* 3s.

THE EARTH. An Introduction to Physiography. By EVAN SMALL, M.A. *Illustrated.*

INSECT LIFE. By F. W. THEOBALD, M.A. *Illustrated.*

ENGLISH POETRY FROM BLAKE TO BROWNING. By W. M. DIXON, M.A.

ENGLISH LOCAL GOVERNMENT. By E. JENKS, M.A., Professor of Law at University College, Liverpool.

THE GREEK VIEW OF LIFE. By G. L. DICKINSON, Fellow of King's College, Cambridge. *Second Edition.*

Social Questions of To-day

Edited by H. DE B. GIBBINS, D.Litt., M.A.

Crown 8vo. 2s. 6d.

A series of volumes upon those topics of social, economic, and industrial interest that are at the present moment foremost in the public mind. Each volume of the series is written by an author who is an acknowledged authority upon the subject with which he deals.

The following Volumes of the Series are ready :—

TRADE UNIONISM—NEW AND OLD. By G. HOWELL. *Second Edition.*

THE CO-OPERATIVE MOVEMENT TO-DAY. By G. J. HOLYOAKE, *Second Edition.*

MUTUAL THRIFT. By Rev. J. FROME WILKINSON, M.A.

PROBLEMS OF POVERTY. By J. A. HOBSON, M.A. *Third Edition.*

THE COMMERCE OF NATIONS. By C. F. BASTABLE, M.A., Professor of Economics at Trinity College, Dublin. *Second Edition.*

THE ALIEN INVASION. By W. H. WILKINS, B.A.

THE RURAL EXODUS. By P. ANDERSON GRAHAM.

LAND NATIONALIZATION. By HAROLD COX, B.A.

A SHORTER WORKING DAY. By H. DE B. GIBBINS, D.Litt., M.A., and R. A. HADFIELD, of the Hecla Works, Sheffield.

BACK TO THE LAND: An Inquiry into the Cure for Rural Depopulation. By H. E. MOORE.

TRUSTS, POOLS AND CORNERS. By J. STEPHEN JEANS.

THE FACTORY SYSTEM. By R. W. COOKE-TAYLOR.

THE STATE AND ITS CHILDREN. By GERTRUDE TUCKWELL.

WOMEN'S WORK. By LADY DILKE, Miss BULLEY, and Miss WHITLEY.

MUNICIPALITIES AT WORK. The Municipal Policy of Six Great Towns, and its Influence on their Social Welfare. By FREDERICK DOLMAN.

SOCIALISM AND MODERN THOUGHT. By M. KAUFMANN.

THE HOUSING OF THE WORKING CLASSES. By E. BOWMAKER.

MODERN CIVILIZATION IN SOME OF ITS ECONOMIC ASPECTS. By W. CUNNINGHAM, D.D., Fellow of Trinity College, Cambridge.
THE PROBLEM OF THE UNEMPLOYED. By J. A. HOBSON, B.A.,
LIFE IN WEST LONDON. By ARTHUR SHERWELL, M.A. *Second Edition.*
RAILWAY NATIONALIZATION. By CLEMENT EDWARDS.
WORKHOUSES AND PAUPERISM. By LOUISA TWINING.

Classical Translations

Edited by H. F. FOX, M.A., Fellow and Tutor of Brasenose College, Oxford.

ÆSCHYLUS—Agamemnon, Chöephoroe, Eumenides. Translated by LEWIS CAMPBELL, LL.D., late Professor of Greek at St. Andrews. 5s.

CICERO—De Oratore I. Translated by E. N. P. MOOR, M.A. 3s. 6d.

CICERO — Select Orations (Pro Milone, Pro Murena, Philippic II., In Catilinam). Translated by H. E. D. BLAKISTON, M.A., Fellow and Tutor of Trinity College, Oxford. 5s.

CICERO—De Natura Deorum. Translated by F. BROOKS, M.A., late Scholar of Balliol College, Oxford. 3s. 6d.

HORACE: THE ODES AND EPODES. Translated by A. GODLEY, M.A., Fellow of Magdalen College, Oxford. 2s.

LUCIAN—Six Dialogues (Nigrinus, Icaro-Menippus, The Cock, The Ship, The Parasite, The Lover of Falsehood). Translated by S. T. IRWIN, M.A., Assistant Master at Clifton; late Scholar of Exeter College, Oxford. 3s. 6d.

SOPHOCLES—Electra and Ajax. Translated by E. D. A. MORSHEAD, M.A., Assistant Master at Winchester. 2s. 6d.

TACITUS—Agricola and Germania. Translated by R. B. TOWNSHEND, late Scholar of Trinity College, Cambridge. 2s. 6d.

Educational Books

CLASSICAL

PLAUTI BACCHIDES. Edited with Introduction, Commentary, and Critical Notes by J. M'COSH, M.A. *Fcap. 4to.* 12s. 6d.
'The notes are copious, and contain a great deal of information that is good and useful.'—*Classical Review.*

PASSAGES FOR UNSEEN TRANSLATION. By E. C. MARCHANT, M.A., Fellow of Peterhouse, Cambridge; and A. M. COOK, M.A., late Scholar of Wadham College, Oxford; Assistant Masters at St. Paul's School. *Crown 8vo.* 3s. 6d.
'A capital selection, and of more variety and value than such books usually are.'—*Athenæum.*
'A judiciously compiled book which will be found widely convenient.'—*Schoolmaster.*
'We know no book of this class better fitted for use in the higher forms of schools.'—*Guardian.*

TACITI AGRICOLA. With Introduction, Notes, Map, etc. By R. F. DAVIS, M.A., Assistant Master at Weymouth College. *Crown 8vo.* 2s.

TACITI GERMANIA. By the same Editor. *Crown 8vo.* 2s.

HERODOTUS: EASY SELECTIONS. With Vocabulary. By A. C. LIDDELL, M.A. *Fcap. 8vo.* 1s. 6d.

SELECTIONS FROM THE ODYSSEY. By E. D. STONE, M.A., late Assistant Master at Eton. *Fcap. 8vo.* 1s. 6d.

PLAUTUS: THE CAPTIVI. Adapted for Lower Forms by J. H. FREESE, M.A., late Fellow of St. John's, Cambridge. 1s. 6d.

DEMOSTHENES AGAINST CONON AND CALLICLES. Edited with Notes and Vocabulary, by F. DARWIN SWIFT, M.A., formerly Scholar of Queen's College, Oxford. *Fcap. 8vo.* 2s.

EXERCISES IN LATIN ACCIDENCE. By S. E. WINBOLT, Assistant Master in Christ's Hospital. *Crown 8vo.* 1s. 6d.

An elementary book adapted for Lower Forms to accompany the shorter Latin primer.
'Skilfully arranged.'—*Glasgow Herald.*
'Accurate and well arranged.'—*Athenæum.*

NOTES ON GREEK AND LATIN SYNTAX. By G. BUCKLAND GREEN, M.A., Assistant Master at Edinburgh Academy, late Fellow of St. John's College, Oxon. *Crown 8vo.* 3s. 6d.

Notes and explanations on the chief difficulties of Greek and Latin Syntax, with numerous passages for exercise.
'Supplies a gap in educational literature.'—*Glasgow Herald.*

GERMAN

A COMPANION GERMAN GRAMMAR. By H. DE B. GIBBINS, D.Litt., M.A., Assistant Master at Nottingham High School. *Crown 8vo.* 1s. 6d.

GERMAN PASSAGES FOR UNSEEN TRANSLATION. By E. M'QUEEN GRAY. *Crown 8vo.* 2s. 6d.

SCIENCE

THE WORLD OF SCIENCE. Including Chemistry, Heat, Light, Sound, Magnetism, Electricity, Botany, Zoology, Physiology, Astronomy, and Geology. By R. ELLIOTT STEEL, M.A., F.C.S. 147 Illustrations. *Second Edition. Crown 8vo.* 2s. 6d.

ELEMENTARY LIGHT. By R. E. STEEL. With numerous Illustrations. *Crown 8vo.* 4s. 6d.

ENGLISH

ENGLISH RECORDS. A Companion to the History of England. By H. E. MALDEN, M.A. *Crown 8vo.* 3s. 6d.

A book which aims at concentrating information upon dates, genealogy, officials, constitutional documents, etc., which is usually found scattered in different volumes.

THE ENGLISH CITIZEN: HIS RIGHTS AND DUTIES. By H. E. MALDEN, M.A. 1s. 6d.

A DIGEST OF DEDUCTIVE LOGIC. By JOHNSON BARKER, B.A. *Crown 8vo.* 2s. 6d.

TEST CARDS IN EUCLID AND ALGEBRA. By D. S. CALDERWOOD, Headmaster of the Normal School, Edinburgh. In three packets of 40, with Answers. 1s.

A set of cards for advanced pupils in elementary schools.

'They bear all the marks of having been prepared by a teacher of experience who knows the value of careful grading and constant repetition. Sums are specially inserted to meet all likely difficulties. The papers set at the various public examinations have been largely drawn upon in preparing the cards.'—*Glasgow Herald.*

METHUEN'S COMMERCIAL SERIES

Edited by H. DE B. GIBBINS, D.Litt., M.A.

BRITISH COMMERCE AND COLONIES FROM ELIZABETH TO VICTORIA. By H. DE B. GIBBINS, D.Litt., M.A. 2s. *Third Edition.*

COMMERCIAL EXAMINATION PAPERS. By H. DE B. GIBBINS, D.Litt., M.A., 1s. 6d.

THE ECONOMICS OF COMMERCE. By H. DE B. GIBBINS, D.Litt., M.A. 1s. 6d.

FRENCH COMMERCIAL CORRESPONDENCE. By S. E. BALLY, Modern Language Master at the Manchester Grammar School. 2s. *Second Edition.*

GERMAN COMMERCIAL CORRESPONDENCE. By S. E. BALLY, 2s. 6d.

A FRENCH COMMERCIAL READER. By S. E. BALLY. 2s.

COMMERCIAL GEOGRAPHY, with special reference to the British Empire. By L. W. LYDE, M.A., of the Academy, Glasgow. 2s. *Second Edition.*

A PRIMER OF BUSINESS. By S. JACKSON, M.A. 1s. 6d. *Second Edition.*

COMMERCIAL ARITHMETIC. By F. G. TAYLOR, M.A. *Second Edition.* 1s. 6d.

PRÉCIS WRITING AND OFFICE CORRESPONDENCE. By E. E. WHITFIELD, M.A. 2s.

WORKS BY A. M. M. STEDMAN, M.A.

INITIA LATINA: Easy Lessons on Elementary Accidence. *Third Edition.* Fcap. 8vo. 1s.

FIRST LATIN LESSONS. *Fifth Edition.* Crown 8vo. 2s.

FIRST LATIN READER. With Notes adapted to the Shorter Latin Primer and Vocabulary. *Fourth Edition revised.* 18mo. 1s. 6d.

EASY SELECTIONS FROM CAESAR. Part I. The Helvetian War. *Second Edition.* 18mo. 1s.

EASY SELECTIONS FROM LIVY. Part I. The Kings of Rome. 18mo. 1s. 6d.

EASY LATIN PASSAGES FOR UNSEEN TRANSLATION. *Fifth Edition.* Fcap. 8vo. 1s. 6d.

EXEMPLA LATINA. First Lessons in Latin Accidence. With Vocabulary. Crown 8vo. 1s.

EASY LATIN EXERCISES ON THE SYNTAX OF THE SHORTER AND REVISED LATIN PRIMER. With Vocabulary. *Seventh and cheaper Edition re-written.* Crown 8vo. 1s. 6d. Issued with the consent of Dr. Kennedy.

THE LATIN COMPOUND SENTENCE: Rules and Exercises. Crown 8vo. 1s. 6d. With Vocabulary. 2s.

NOTANDA QUAEDAM: Miscellaneous Latin Exercises on Common Rules and Idioms. *Third Edition.* Fcap. 8vo. 1s. 6d. With Vocabulary. 2s.

LATIN VOCABULARIES FOR REPETITION: Arranged according to Subjects. *Seventh Edition.* Fcap. 8vo. 1s. 6d.

A VOCABULARY OF LATIN IDIOMS AND PHRASES. 18mo. *Second Edition.* 1s.

STEPS TO GREEK. 18mo. 1s.

A SHORTER GREEK PRIMER. *Crown* 8vo. 1s. 6d.

EASY GREEK PASSAGES FOR UNSEEN TRANSLATION. *Third Edition Revised. Fcap.* 8vo. 1s. 6d.

GREEK VOCABULARIES FOR REPETITION. Arranged according to Subjects. *Second Edition. Fcap.* 8vo. 1s. 6d.

GREEK TESTAMENT SELECTIONS. For the use of Schools. *Third Edition.* With Introduction, Notes, and Vocabulary. *Fcap.* 8vo. 2s. 6d.

STEPS TO FRENCH. *Fourth Edition.* 18mo. 8d.

FIRST FRENCH LESSONS. *Third Edition Revised. Crown* 8vo. 1s.

EASY FRENCH PASSAGES FOR UNSEEN TRANSLATION. *Third Edition revised. Fcap.* 8vo. 1s. 6d.

EASY FRENCH EXERCISES ON ELEMENTARY SYNTAX. With Vocabulary. *Second Edition. Crown* 8vo. 2s. 6d. KEY 3s. *net.*

FRENCH VOCABULARIES FOR REPETITION: Arranged according to Subjects. *Sixth Edition. Fcap.* 8vo. 1s.

SCHOOL EXAMINATION SERIES

EDITED BY A. M. M. STEDMAN, M.A. *Crown* 8vo. 2s. 6d.

FRENCH EXAMINATION PAPERS IN MISCELLANEOUS GRAMMAR AND IDIOMS. By A. M. M. STEDMAN, M.A. *Ninth Edition.*
A KEY, issued to Tutors and Private Students only, to be had on application to the Publishers. *Fourth Edition. Crown* 8vo. 6s. *net.*

LATIN EXAMINATION PAPERS IN MISCELLANEOUS GRAMMAR AND IDIOMS. By A. M. M. STEDMAN, M.A. *Eighth Edition.* KEY (*Third Edition*) issued as above. 6s. *net.*

GREEK EXAMINATION PAPERS IN MISCELLANEOUS GRAMMAR AND IDIOMS. By A. M. M. STEDMAN, M.A. *Fifth Edition.* KEY (*Second Edition*) issued as above. 6s. *net.*

GERMAN EXAMINATION PAPERS IN MISCELLANEOUS GRAMMAR AND IDIOMS. By R. J. MORICH, Manchester. *Fifth Edition.* KEY (*Second Edition*) issued as above. 6s. *net.*

HISTORY AND GEOGRAPHY EXAMINATION PAPERS. By C. H. SPENCE, M.A., Clifton College. *Second Edition.*

SCIENCE EXAMINATION PAPERS. By R. E. STEEL, M.A., F.C.S., Chief Natural Science Master, Bradford Grammar School. *In two vols.* Part I. Chemistry; Part II. Physics.

GENERAL KNOWLEDGE EXAMINATION PAPERS. By A. M. M. STEDMAN, M.A. *Third Edition.*
KEY (*Second Edition*) issued as above. 7s. *net.*

www.ingramcontent.com/pod-product-compliance
Lightning Source LLC
Chambersburg PA
CBHW030819230426
43667CB00008B/1281